For Mum
(soz about the swearing

To Jodie, Thanks so much!

ISBN: 978-0-9574318-1-2

House Party
Copyright © 2014 Rachael Smith
All Rights Reserved

www.rachaelsmith.org

GREAT BEAST

xxx

Published by Great Beast Comics
17 Warwick Road, Chorlton, Manchester, M21 0AX, UK
To view our catalogue please visit www.greatbeastcomics.com

First edition June 2014
Printed in the UK

PROLOGUE

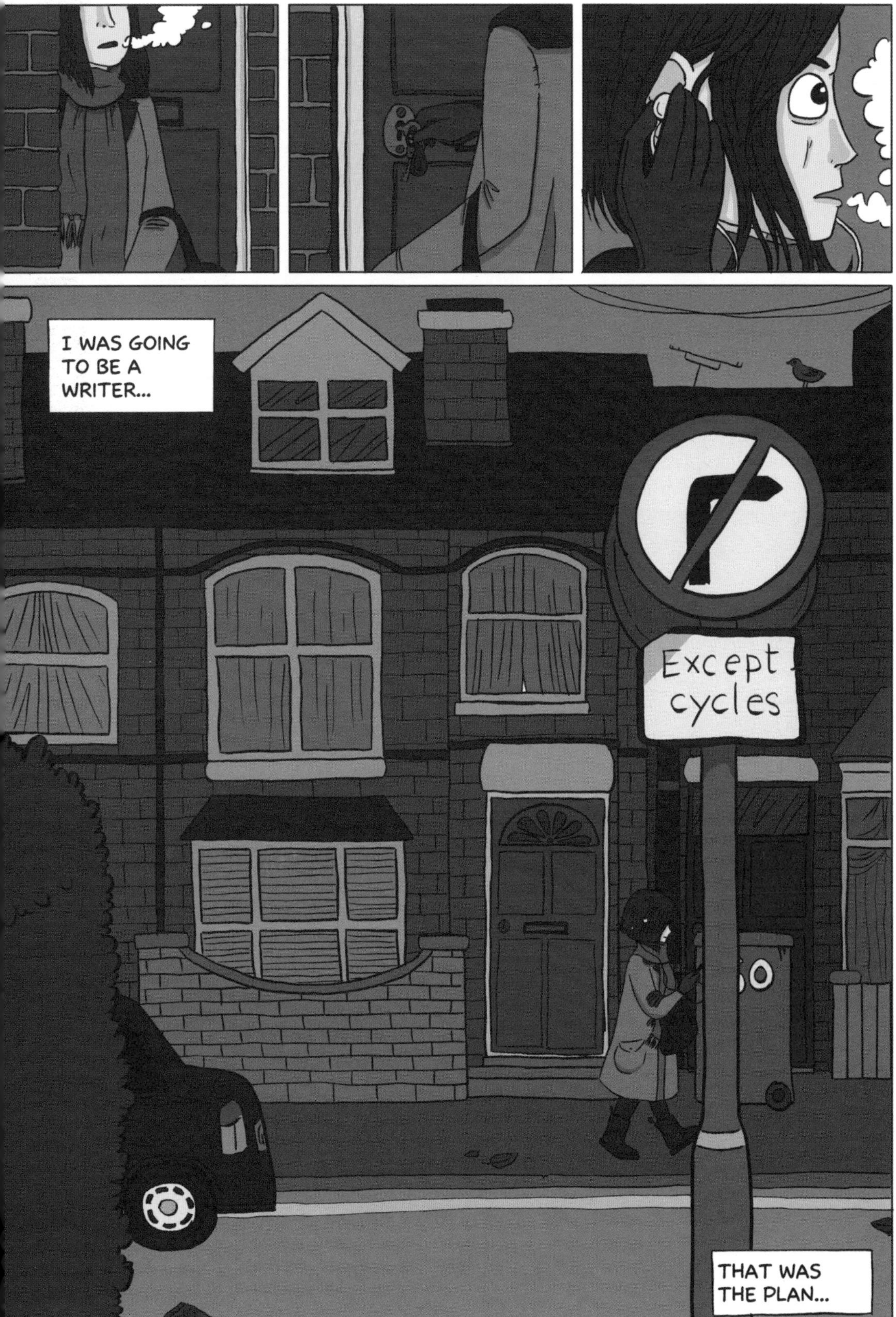
I WAS GOING TO BE A WRITER...
Except cycles
THAT WAS THE PLAN...

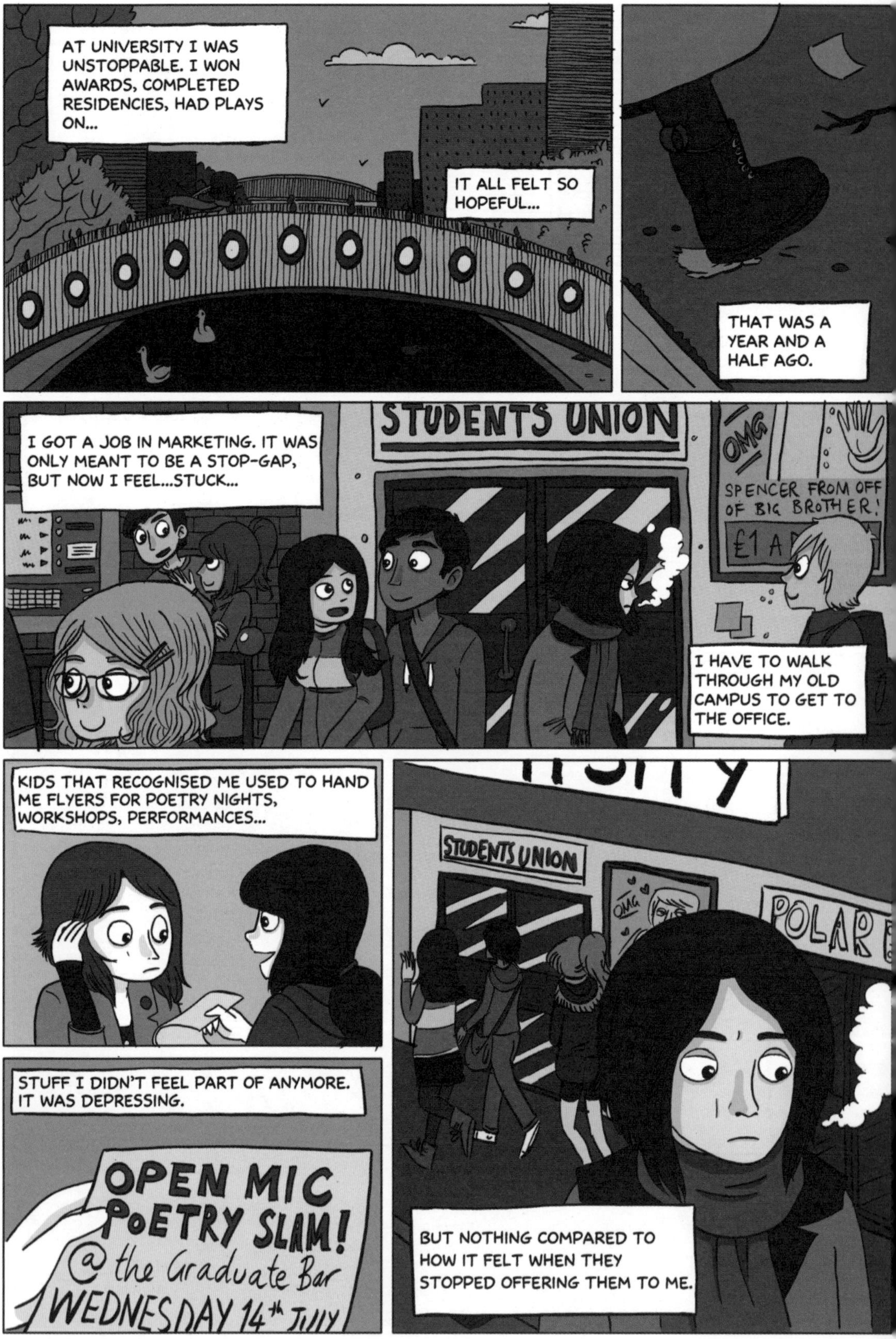
AT UNIVERSITY I WAS UNSTOPPABLE. I WON AWARDS, COMPLETED RESIDENCIES, HAD PLAYS ON...
IT ALL FELT SO HOPEFUL...
THAT WAS A YEAR AND A HALF AGO.
I GOT A JOB IN MARKETING. IT WAS ONLY MEANT TO BE A STOP-GAP, BUT NOW I FEEL...STUCK...
STUDENTS UNION
OMG
SPENCER FROM OFF OF BIG BROTHER!
I HAVE TO WALK THROUGH MY OLD CAMPUS TO GET TO THE OFFICE.
KIDS THAT RECOGNISED ME USED TO HAND ME FLYERS FOR POETRY NIGHTS, WORKSHOPS, PERFORMANCES...
STUDENTS UNION
OMG
STUFF I DIDN'T FEEL PART OF ANYMORE. IT WAS DEPRESSING.
OPEN MIC POETRY SLAM! @ the Graduate Bar WEDNESDAY 14th July
BUT NOTHING COMPARED TO HOW IT FELT WHEN THEY STOPPED OFFERING THEM TO ME.

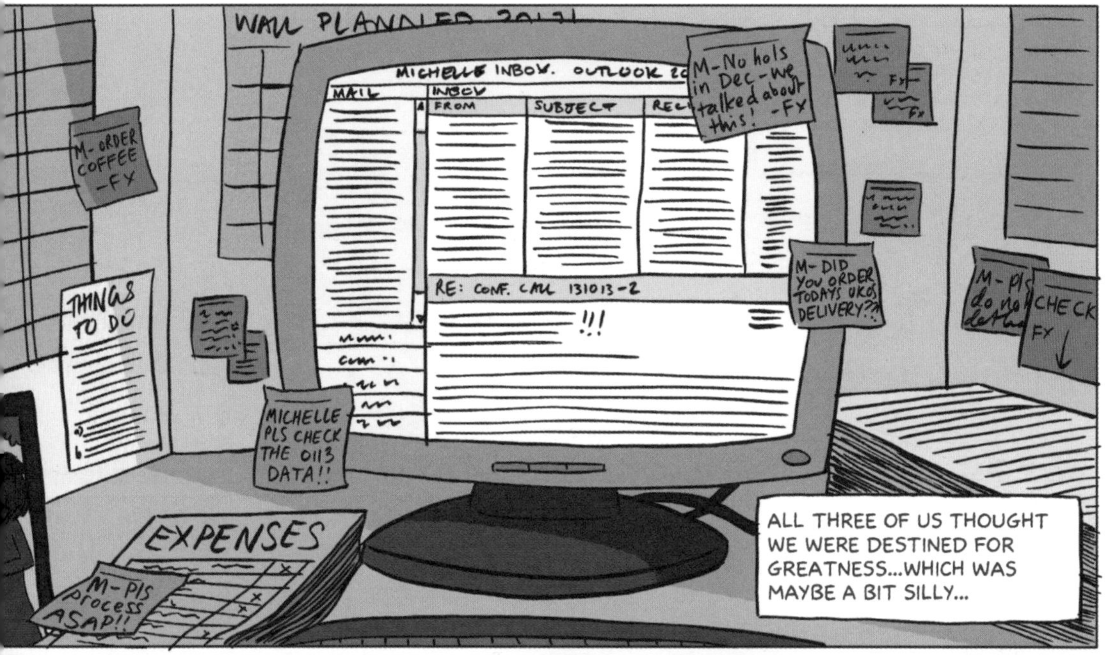
WALL PLANNER
M-No hols in Dec-we talked about this! -FX
M-ORDER COFFEE -FX
THINGS TO DO
RE: CONF. CALL 131013-2
M-DID YOU ORDER TODAYS UKOS DELIVERY??
CHECK FX
MICHELLE PLS CHECK THE 0113 DATA!!
EXPENSES
M-Pls process ASAP!!
ALL THREE OF US THOUGHT WE WERE DESTINED FOR GREATNESS...WHICH WAS MAYBE A BIT SILLY...

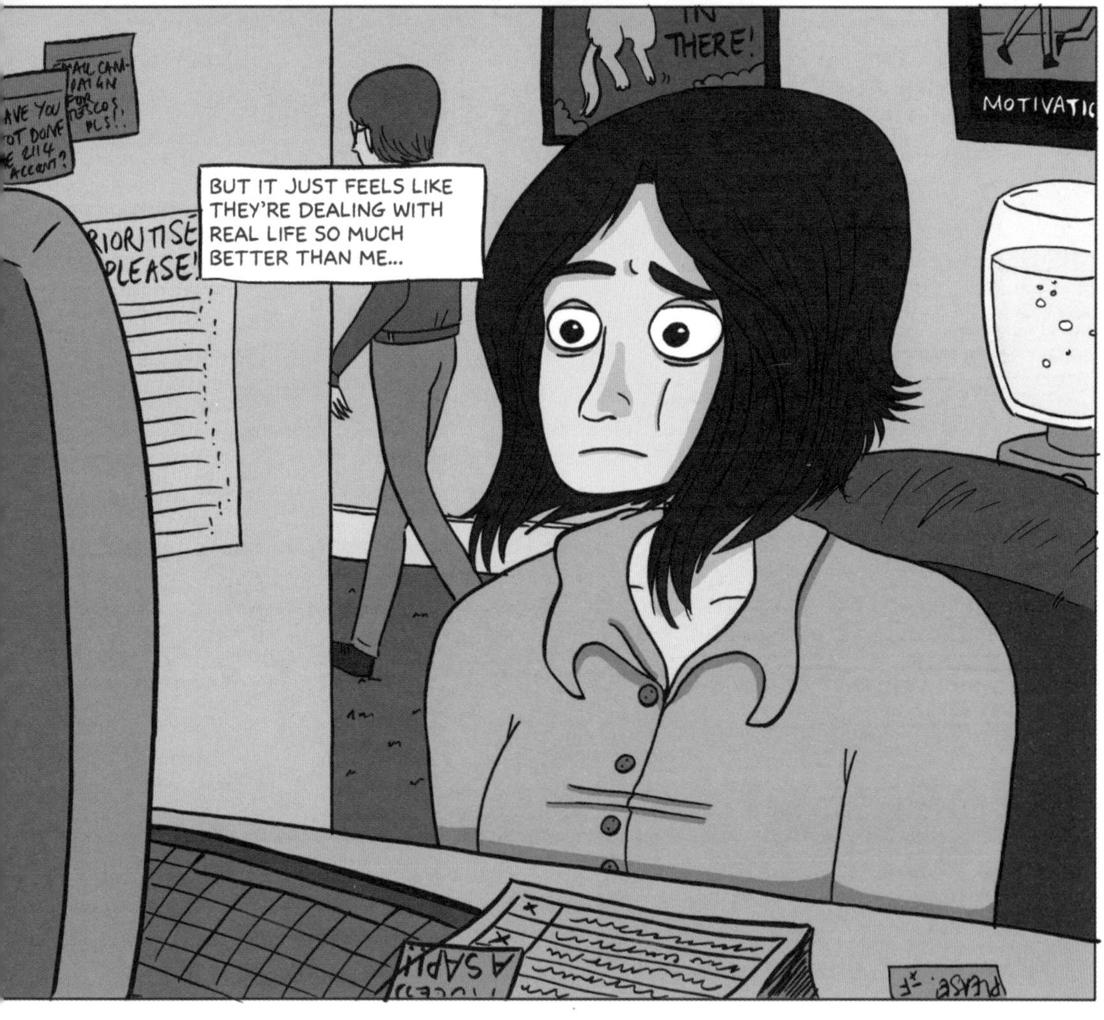
THERE!
BUT IT JUST FEELS LIKE THEY'RE DEALING WITH REAL LIFE SO MUCH BETTER THAN ME...

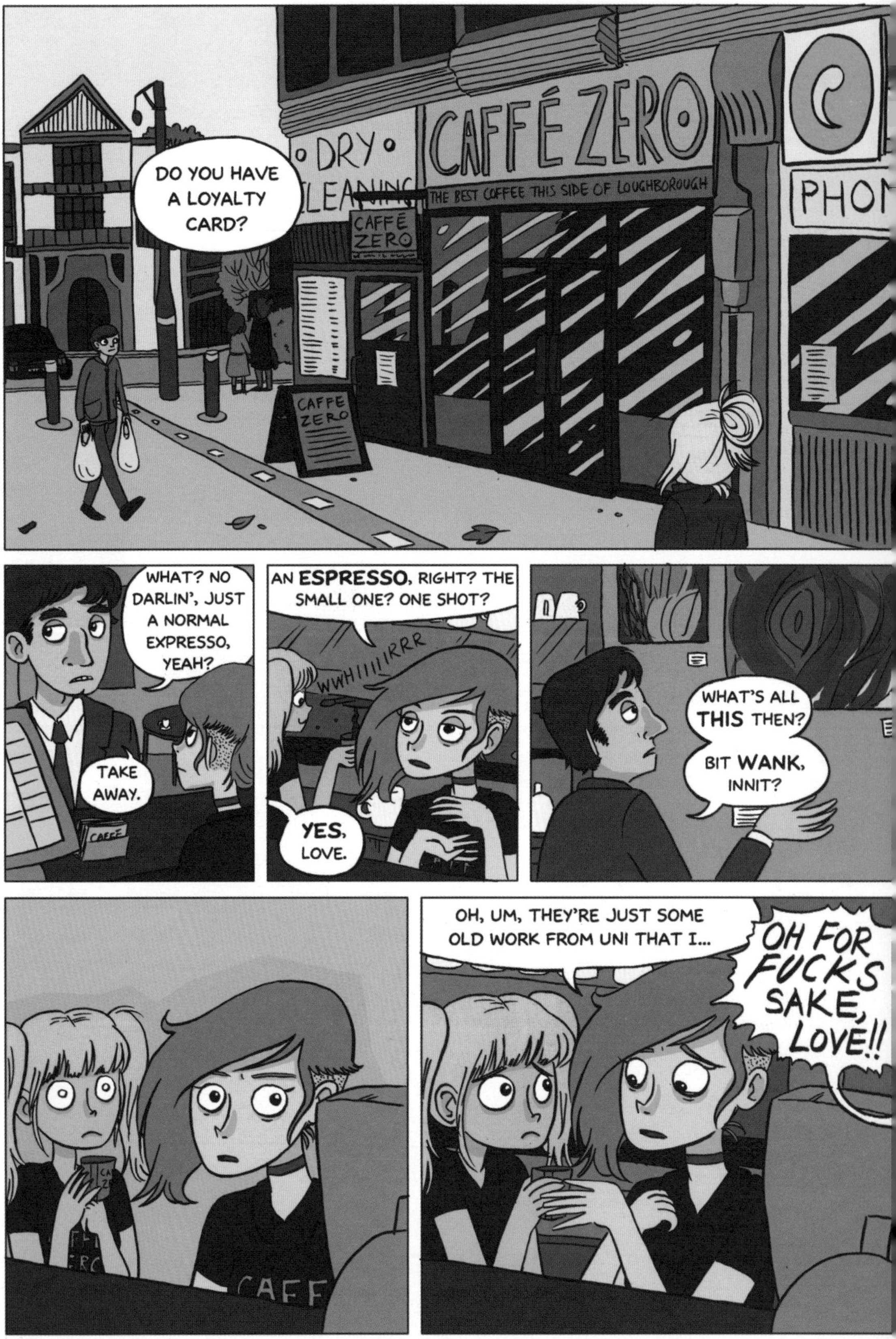
DRY CLEANING
CAFFÉ ZERO
THE BEST COFFEE THIS SIDE OF LOUGHBOROUGH
PHON
CAFFÉ ZERO
CAFFE ZERO
DO YOU HAVE A LOYALTY CARD?
WHAT? NO DARLIN', JUST A NORMAL EXPRESSO, YEAH?
TAKE AWAY.
AN ESPRESSO, RIGHT? THE SMALL ONE? ONE SHOT?
WWHIIIIIRRR
YES, LOVE.
WHAT'S ALL THIS THEN?
BIT WANK, INNIT?
OH, UM, THEY'RE JUST SOME OLD WORK FROM UNI THAT I...
OH FOR FUCKS SAKE, LOVE!!

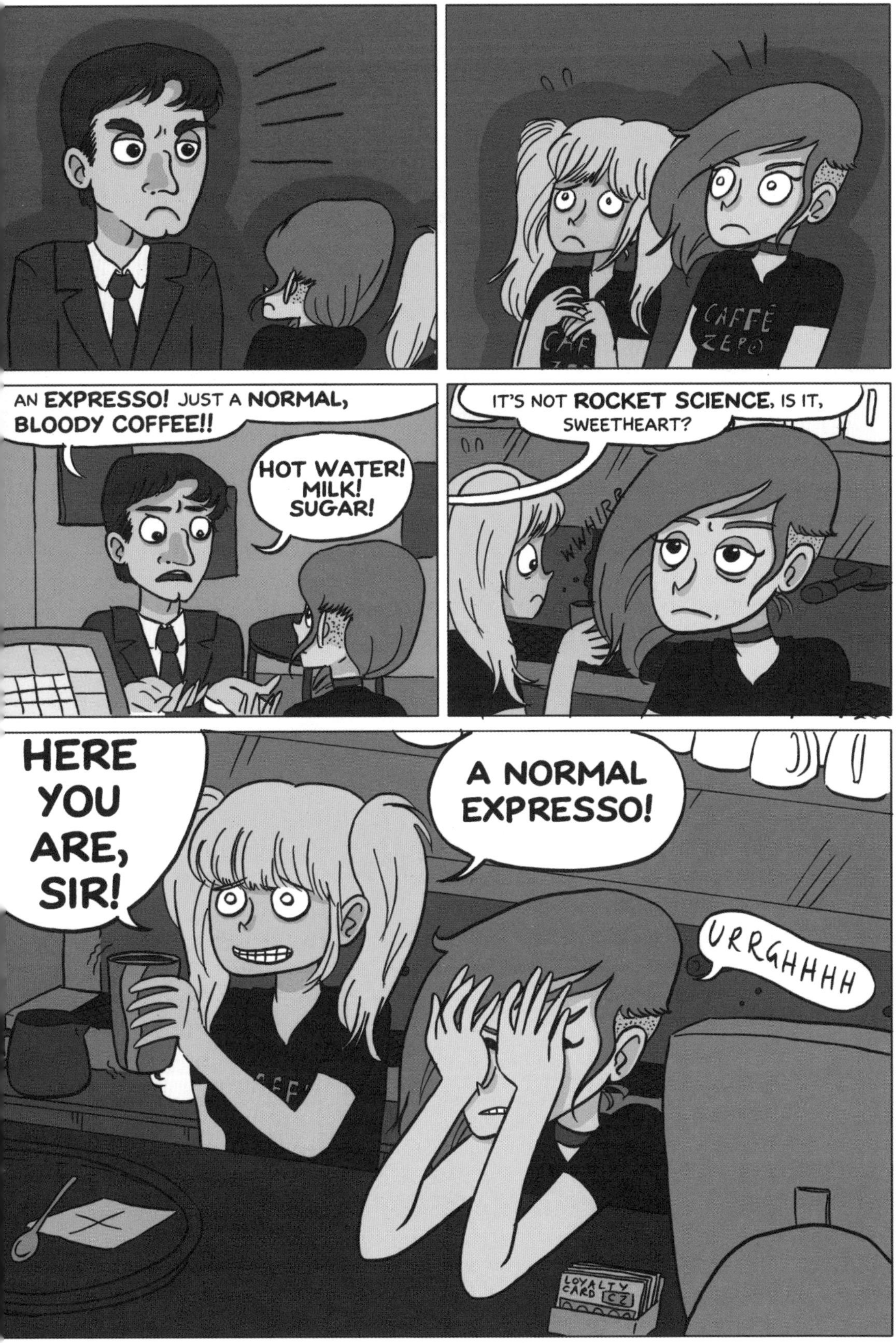

CAFFÈ ZERO
AN EXPRESSO! JUST A NORMAL, BLOODY COFFEE!!
HOT WATER! MILK! SUGAR!
IT'S NOT ROCKET SCIENCE, IS IT, SWEETHEART?
WWHIRR
HERE YOU ARE, SIR!
A NORMAL EXPRESSO!
URRGHHHH
LOYALTY CARD CZ

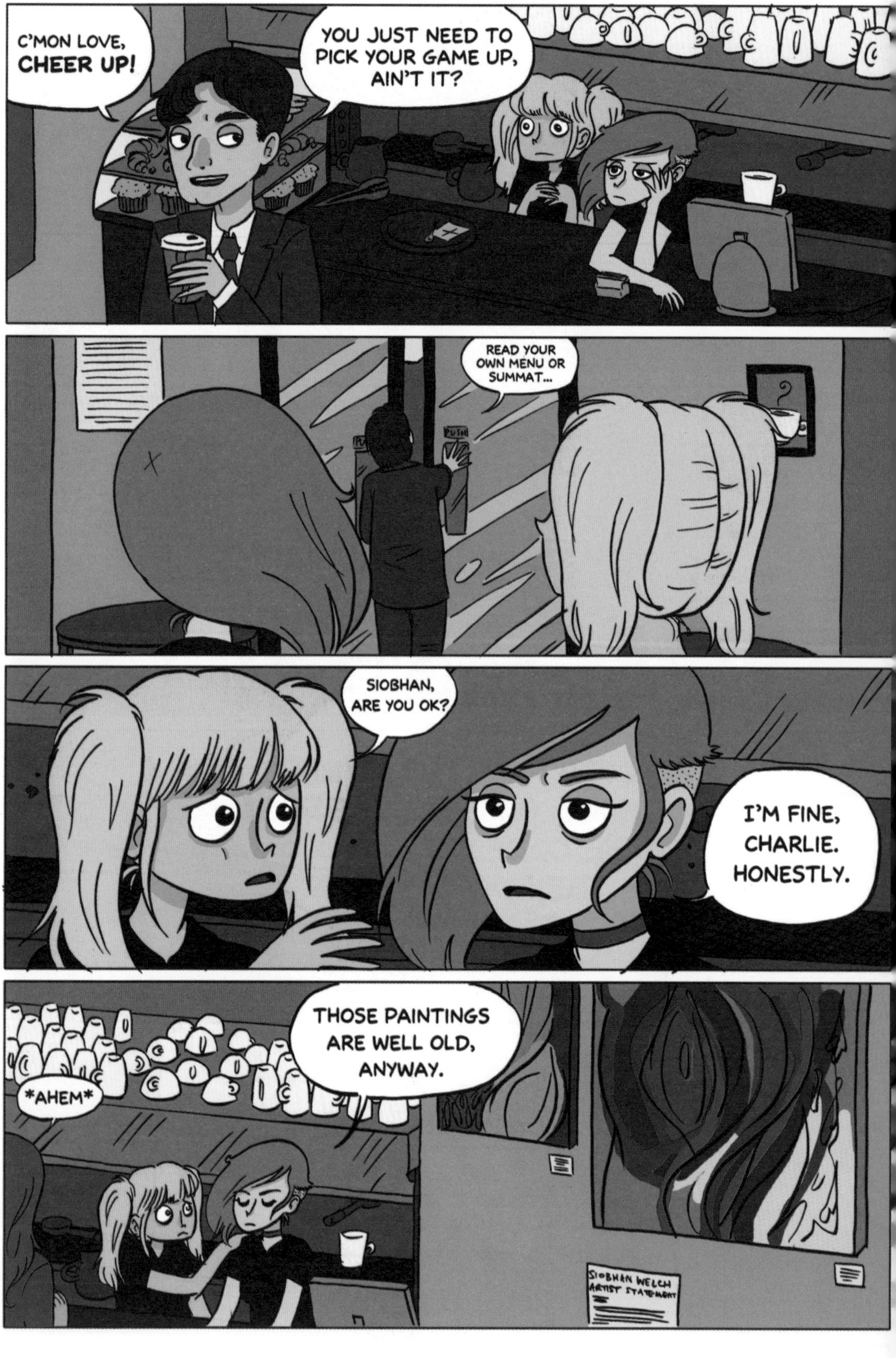
C'MON LOVE, CHEER UP!
YOU JUST NEED TO PICK YOUR GAME UP, AIN'T IT?
READ YOUR OWN MENU OR SUMMAT...
PUSH
SIOBHAN, ARE YOU OK?
I'M FINE, CHARLIE. HONESTLY.
AHEM
THOSE PAINTINGS ARE WELL OLD, ANYWAY.
SIOBHAN WELCH ARTIST STATEMENT

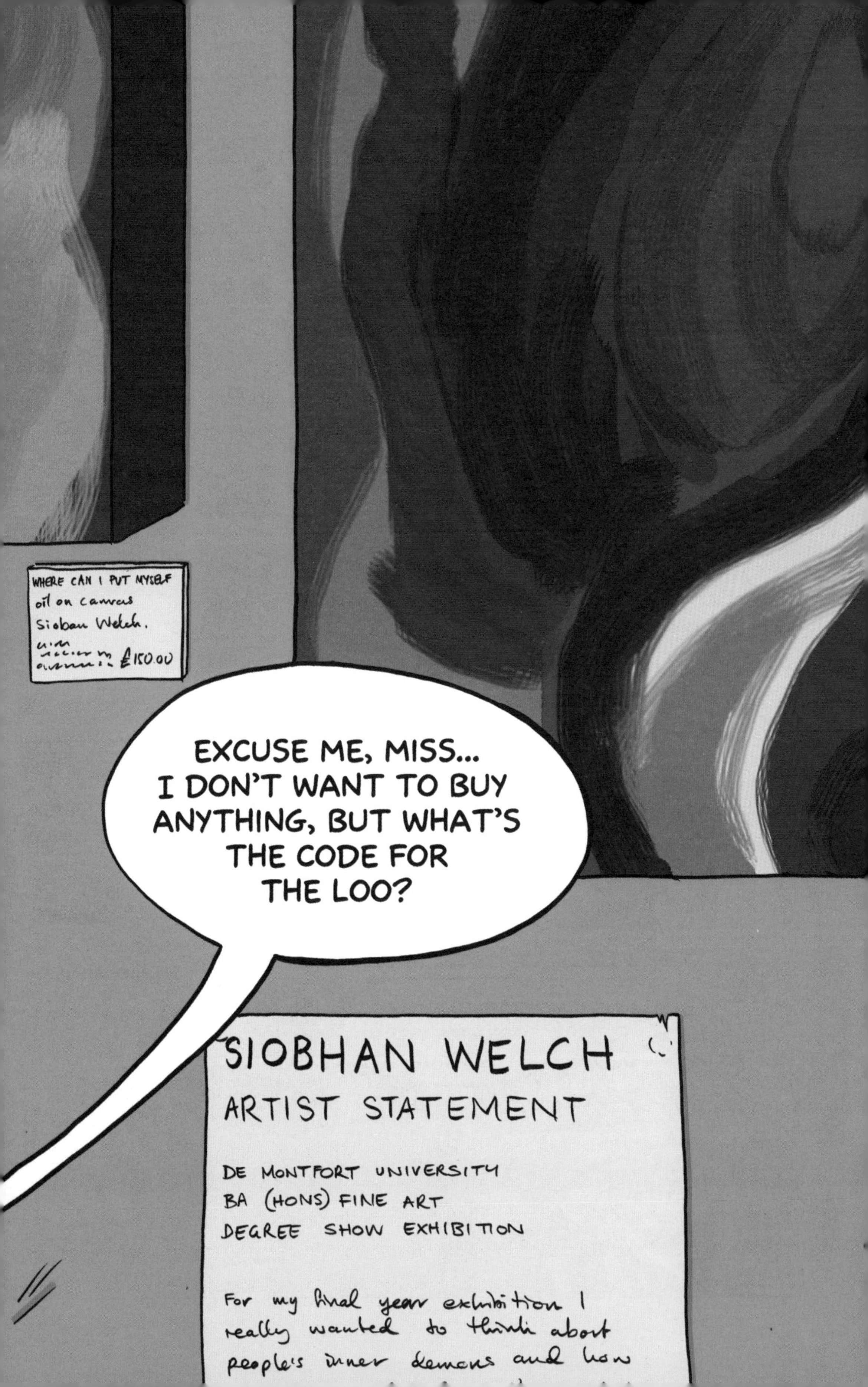
WHERE CAN I PUT MYSELF
oil on canvas
Sioban Welch.
£150.00
EXCUSE ME, MISS... I DON'T WANT TO BUY ANYTHING, BUT WHAT'S THE CODE FOR THE LOO?
SIOBHAN WELCH
ARTIST STATEMENT
DE MONTFORT UNIVERSITY
BA (HONS) FINE ART
DEGREE SHOW EXHIBITION
For my final year exhibition I really wanted to think about people's inner demons and how

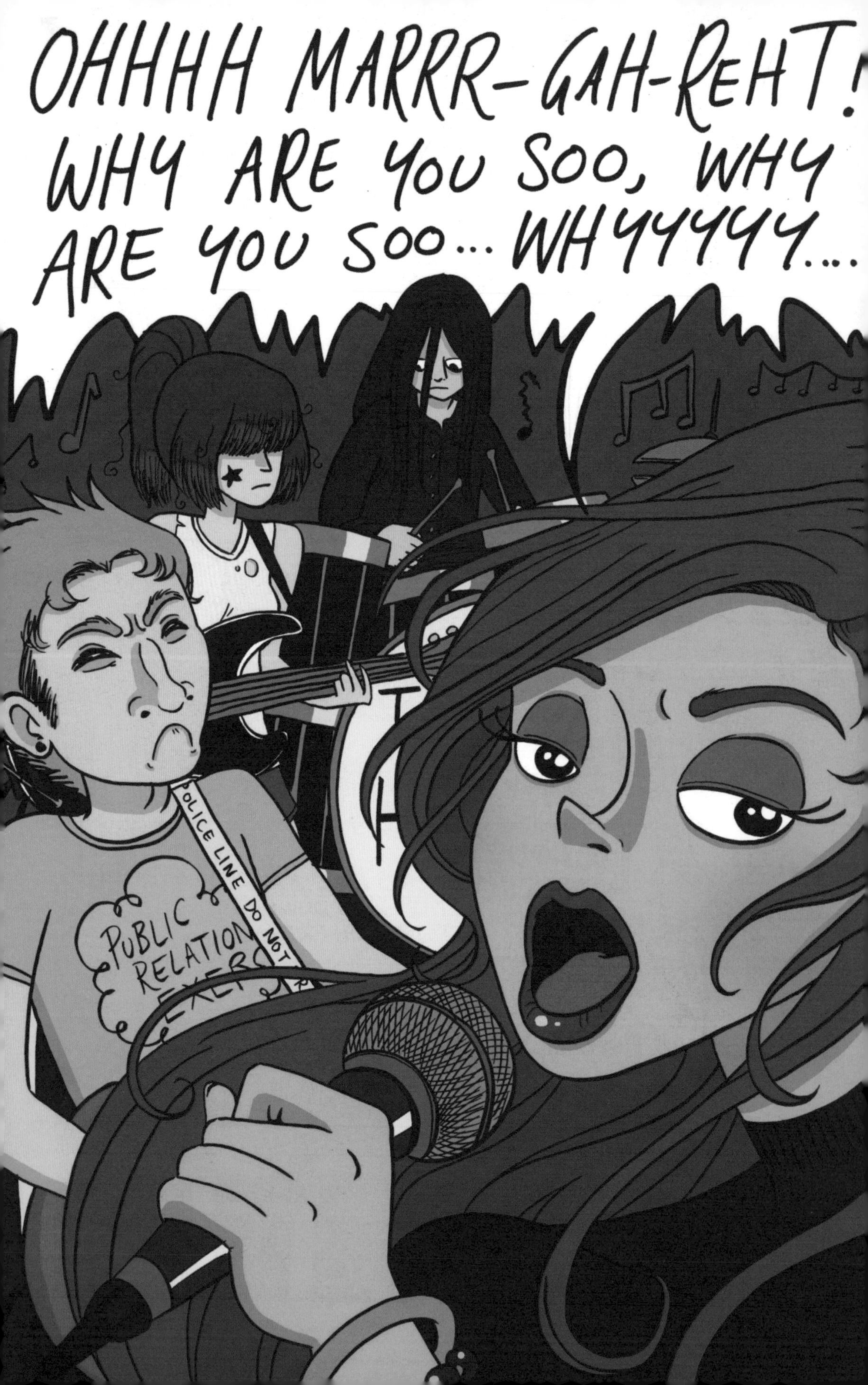
OHHHH MARRR-GAH-REHT!
WHY ARE YOU SOO, WHY ARE YOU SOO... WHYYYYY....
POLICE LINE DO NOT
PUBLIC RELATION

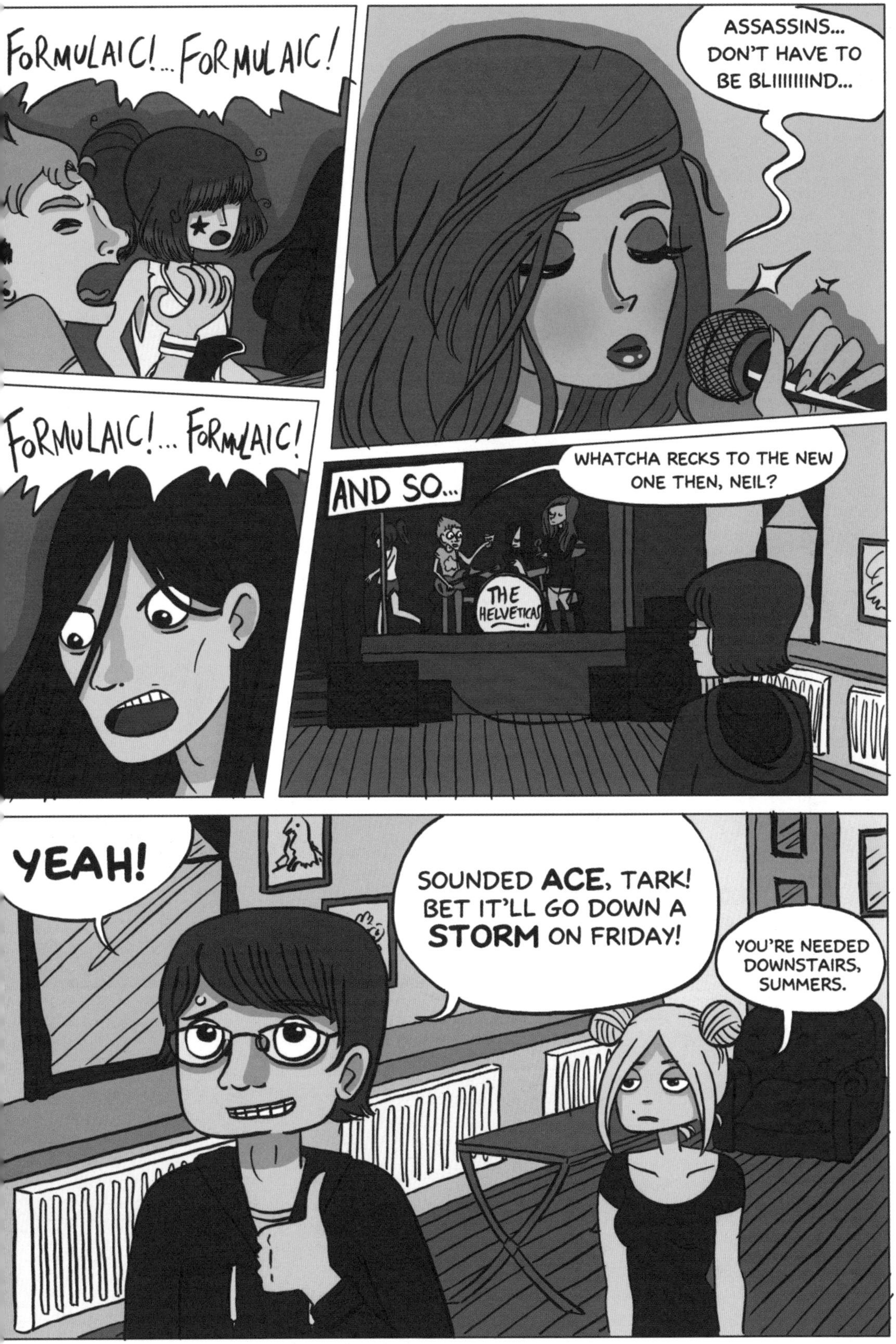
FORMULAIC!... FORMULAIC!
ASSASSINS... DON'T HAVE TO BE BLIIIIIIIND...
FORMULAIC!... FORMULAIC!
AND SO...
WHATCHA RECKS TO THE NEW ONE THEN, NEIL?
THE HELVETICAS
YEAH!
SOUNDED ACE, TARK! BET IT'LL GO DOWN A STORM ON FRIDAY!
YOU'RE NEEDED DOWNSTAIRS, SUMMERS.

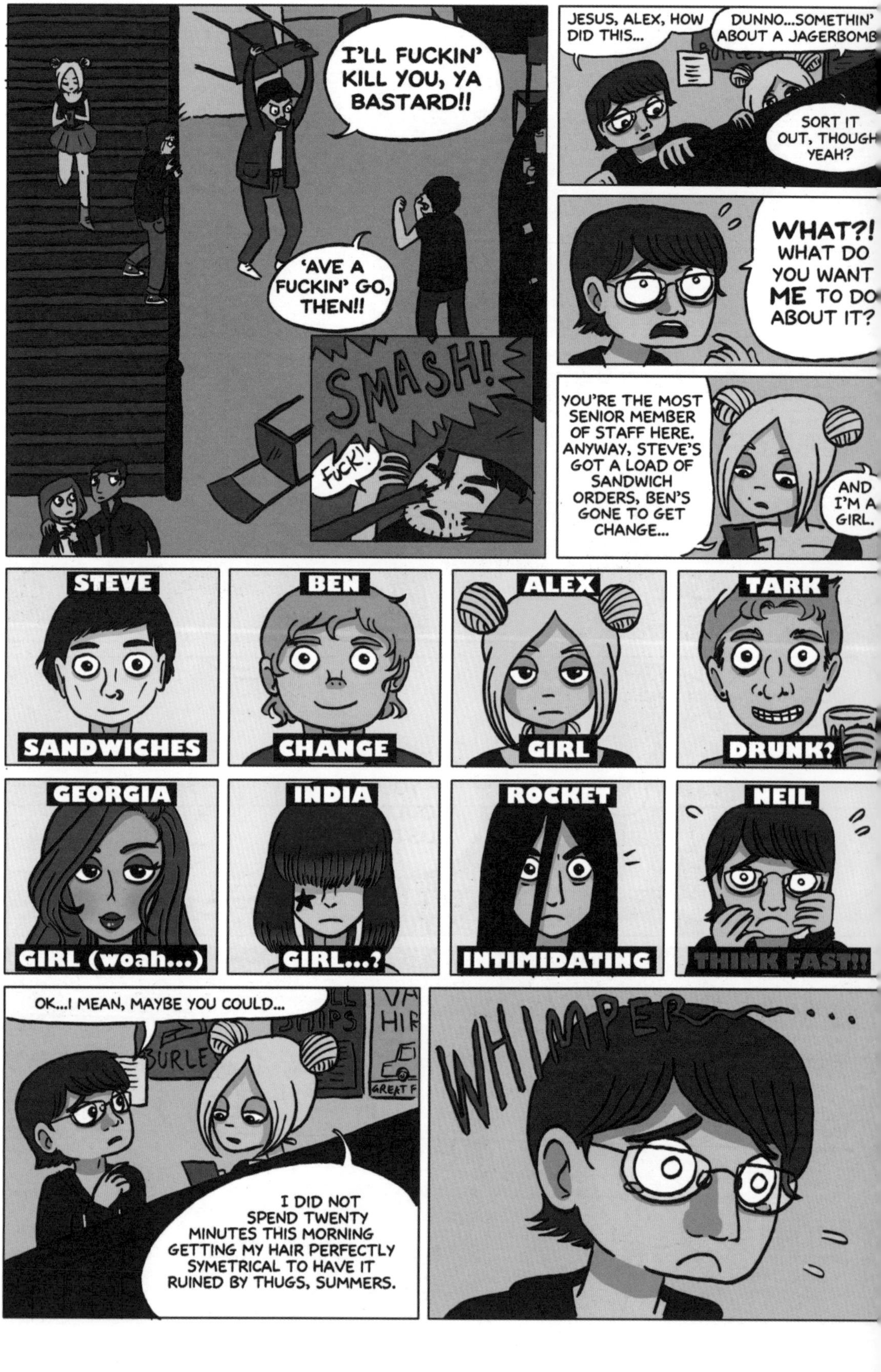
I'LL FUCKIN' KILL YOU, YA BASTARD!!
'AVE A FUCKIN' GO, THEN!!
SMASH!
FUCK!
JESUS, ALEX, HOW DID THIS...
DUNNO...SOMETHIN' ABOUT A JAGERBOMB
SORT IT OUT, THOUGH YEAH?
WHAT?! WHAT DO YOU WANT ME TO DO ABOUT IT?
YOU'RE THE MOST SENIOR MEMBER OF STAFF HERE. ANYWAY, STEVE'S GOT A LOAD OF SANDWICH ORDERS, BEN'S GONE TO GET CHANGE...
AND I'M A GIRL.
STEVE
SANDWICHES
BEN
CHANGE
ALEX
GIRL
TARK
DRUNK?
GEORGIA
GIRL (woah...)
INDIA
GIRL...?
ROCKET
INTIMIDATING
NEIL
THINK FAST!!
OK...I MEAN, MAYBE YOU COULD...
I DID NOT SPEND TWENTY MINUTES THIS MORNING GETTING MY HAIR PERFECTLY SYMETRICAL TO HAVE IT RUINED BY THUGS, SUMMERS.
WHIMPER...

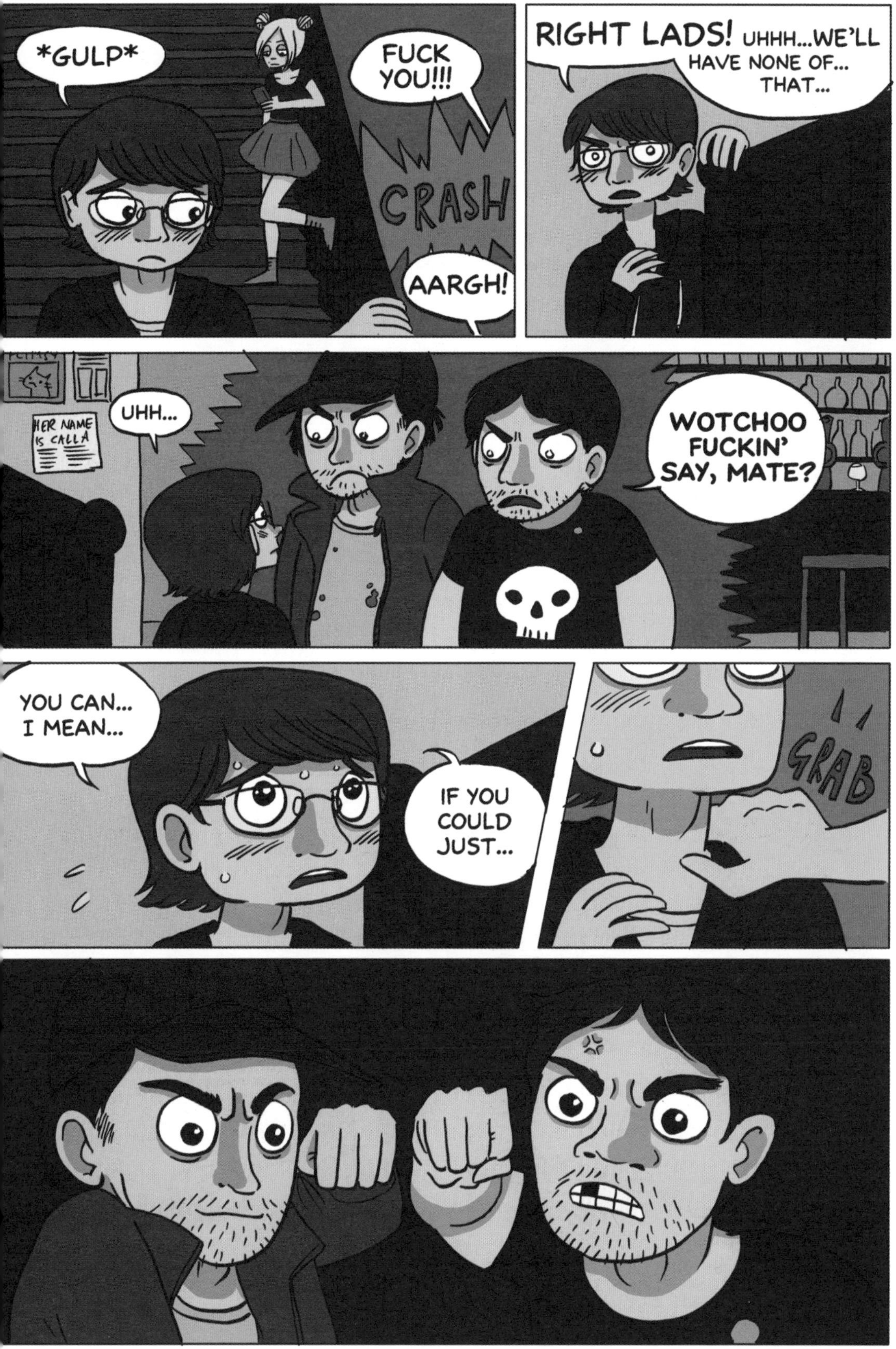
GULP
FUCK YOU!!!
CRASH
AARGH!
RIGHT LADS! UHHH...WE'LL HAVE NONE OF... THAT...
HER NAME IS CALLA
UHH...
WOTCHOO FUCKIN' SAY, MATE?
YOU CAN... I MEAN...
IF YOU COULD JUST...
GRAB

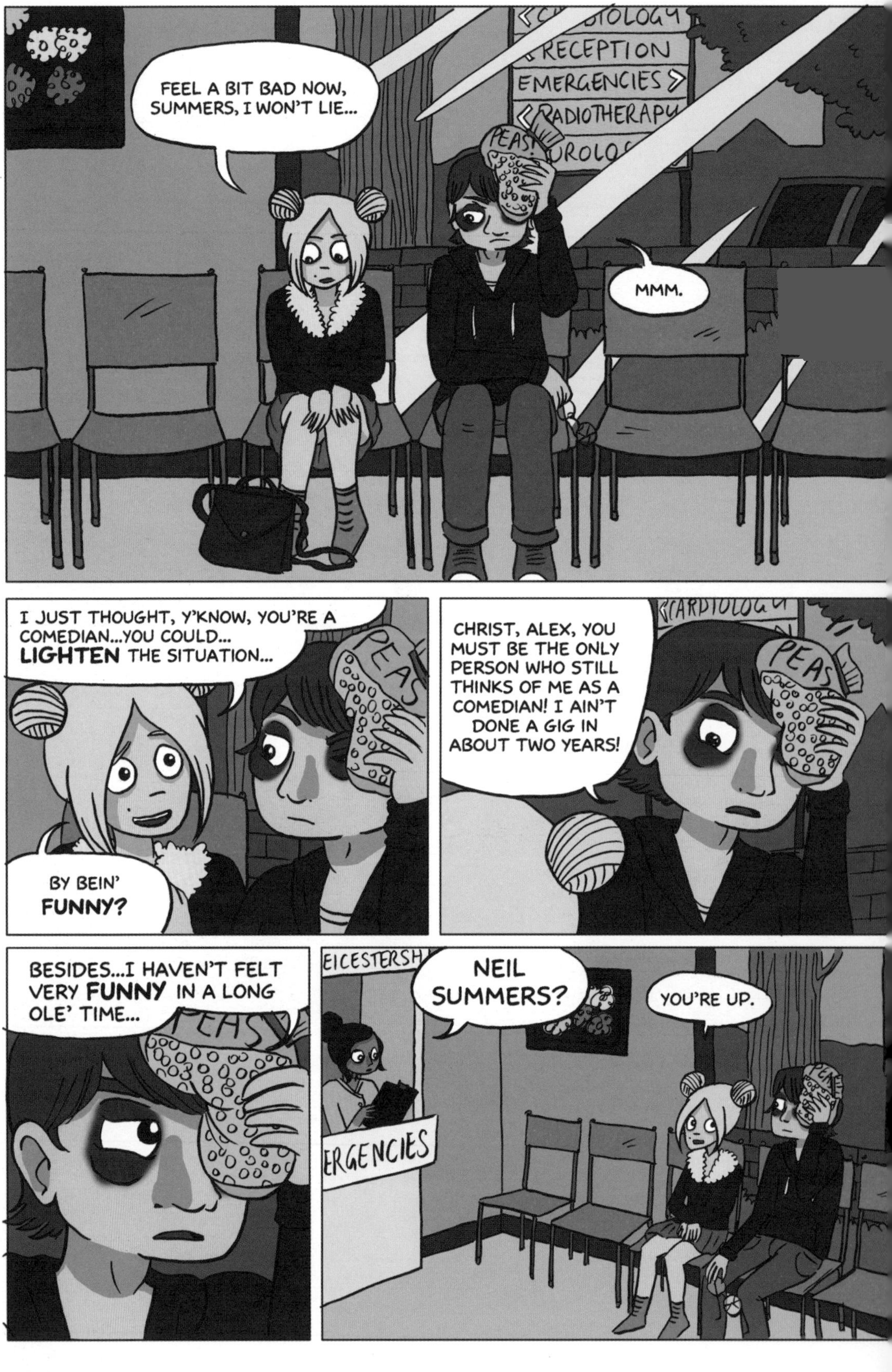

RECEPTION
EMERGENCIES
RADIOTHERAPY
PEAS!
FEEL A BIT BAD NOW, SUMMERS, I WON'T LIE...
MMM.
I JUST THOUGHT, Y'KNOW, YOU'RE A COMEDIAN...YOU COULD... **LIGHTEN** THE SITUATION...
PEAS
BY BEIN' **FUNNY?**
CHRIST, ALEX, YOU MUST BE THE ONLY PERSON WHO STILL THINKS OF ME AS A COMEDIAN! I AIN'T DONE A GIG IN ABOUT TWO YEARS!
PEAS
BESIDES...I HAVEN'T FELT VERY **FUNNY** IN A LONG OLE' TIME...
PEAS
NEIL SUMMERS?
YOU'RE UP.

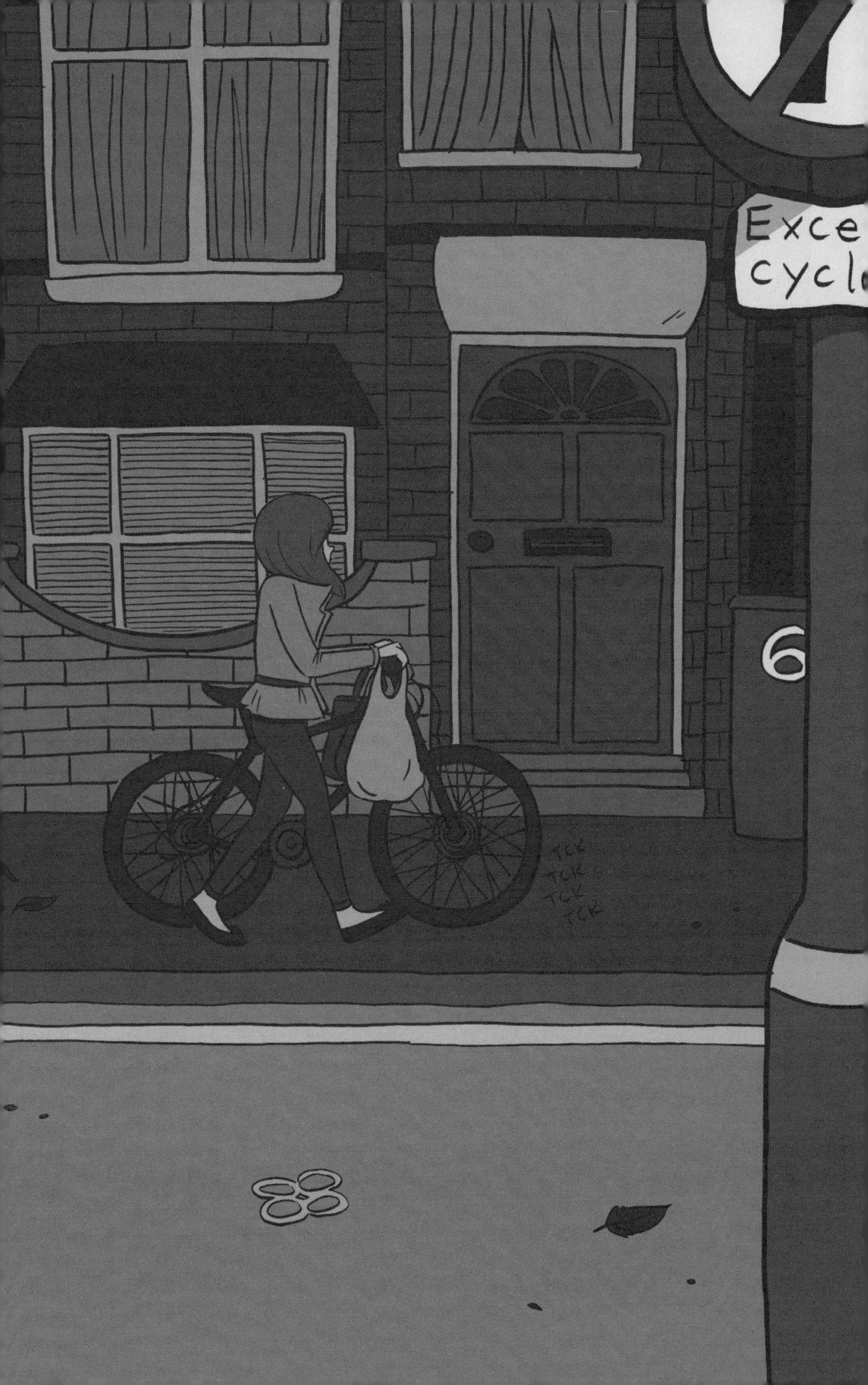
Exce
cycl
6
TCK TCK TCK TCK

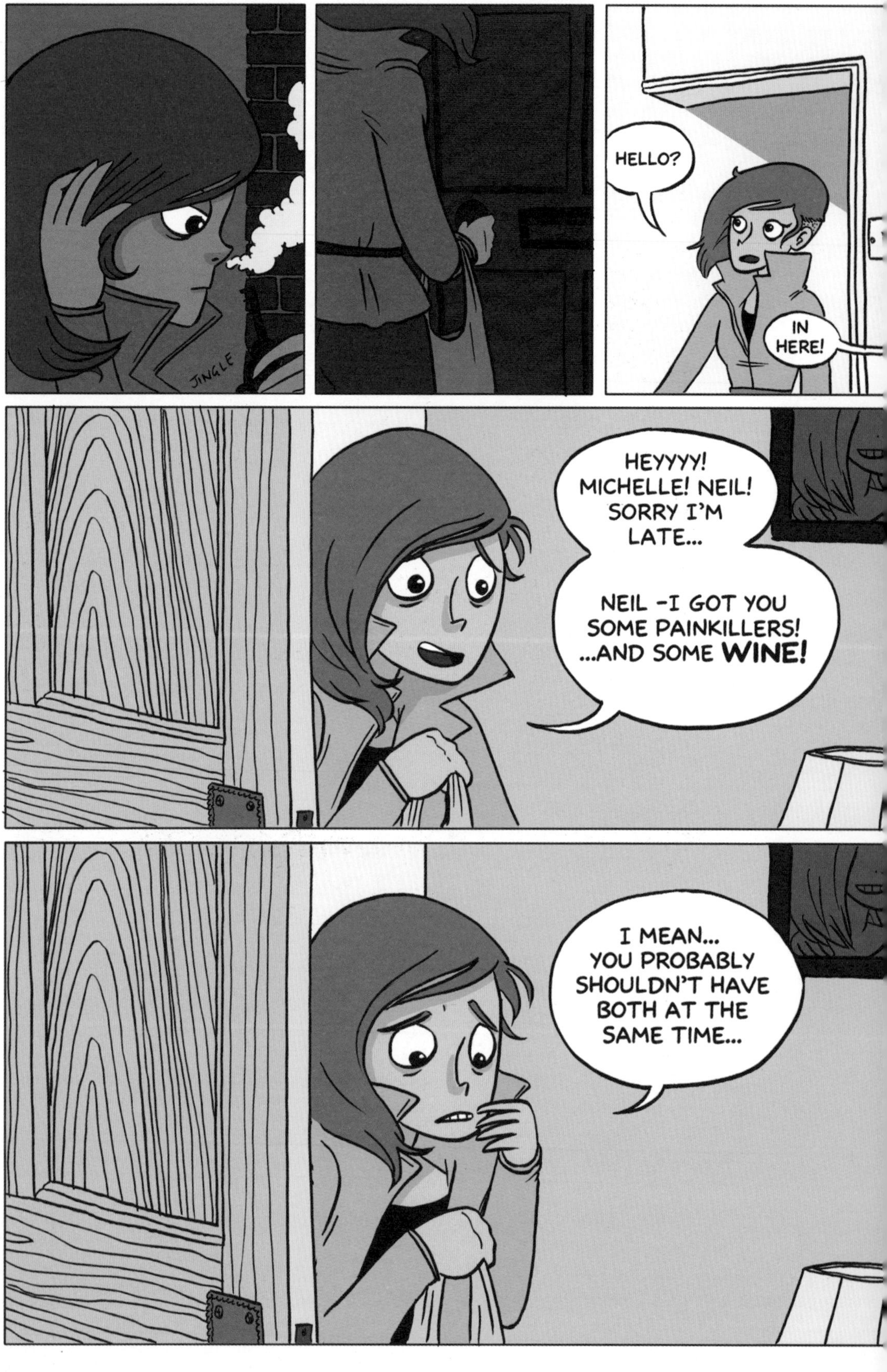
JINGLE
HELLO?
IN HERE!
HEYYYY! MICHELLE! NEIL! SORRY I'M LATE...
NEIL -I GOT YOU SOME PAINKILLERS! ...AND SOME **WINE!**
I MEAN... YOU PROBABLY SHOULDN'T HAVE BOTH AT THE SAME TIME...

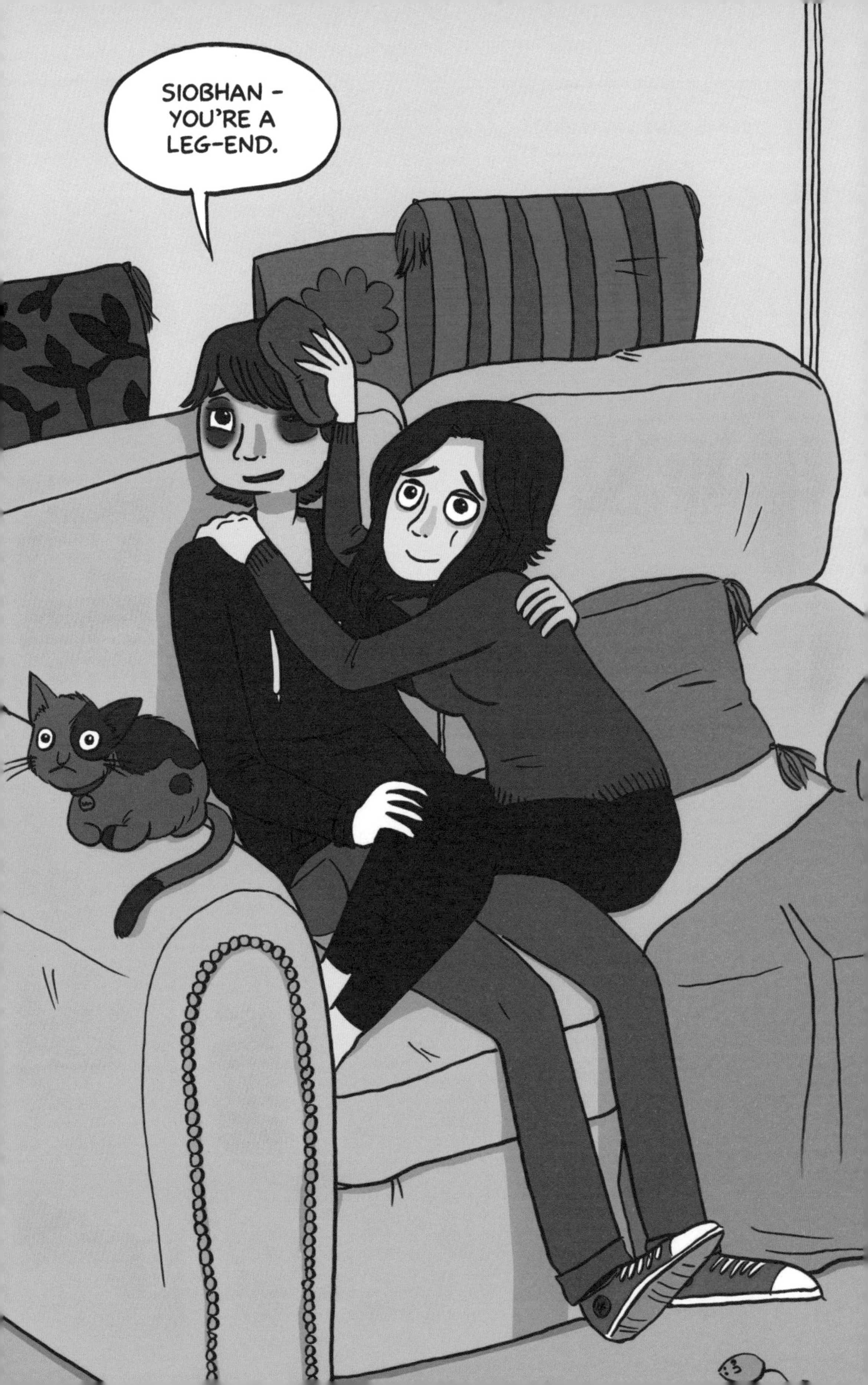
SIOBHAN - YOU'RE A LEG-END.

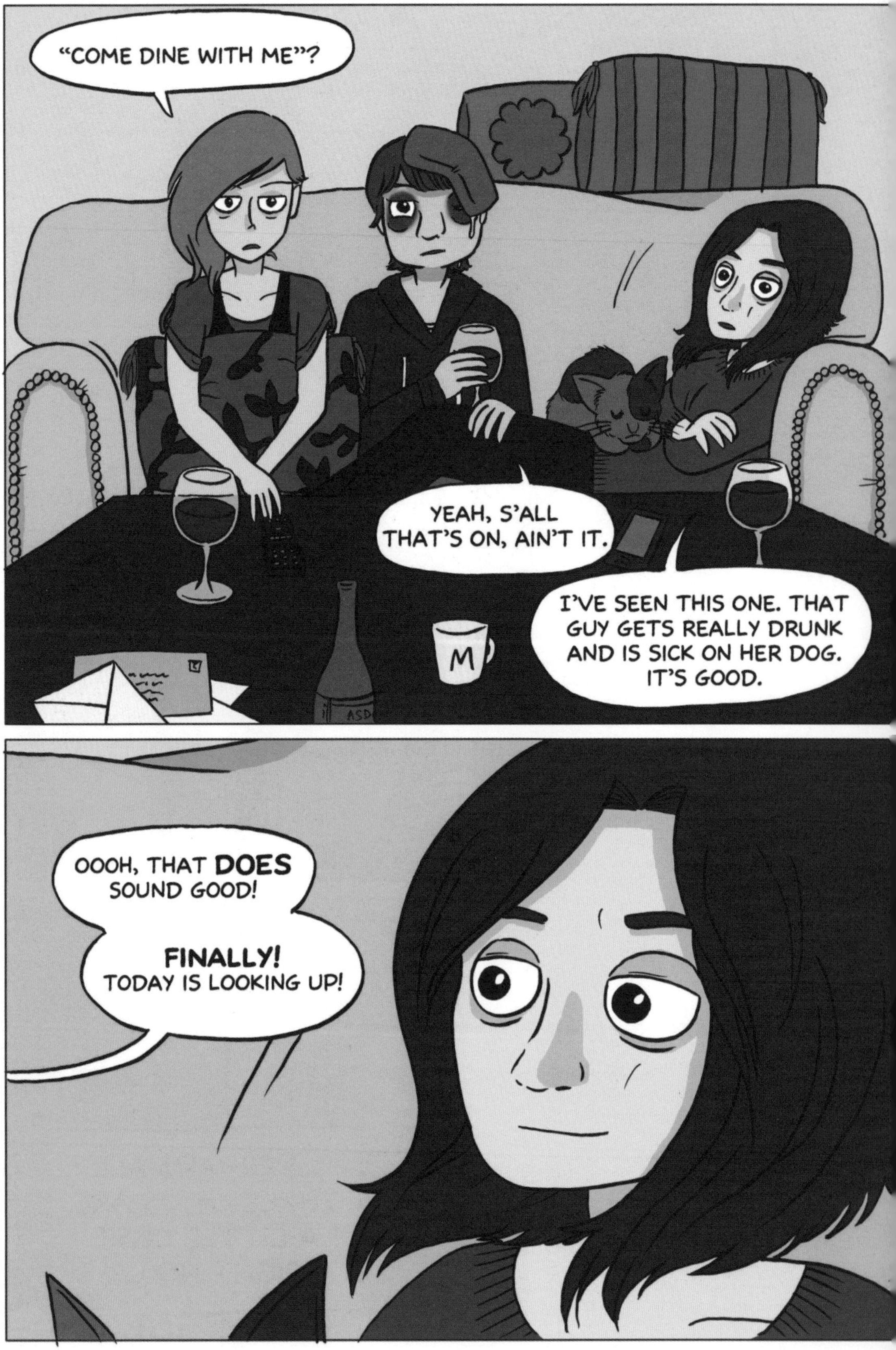
"COME DINE WITH ME"?
YEAH, S'ALL THAT'S ON, AIN'T IT.
I'VE SEEN THIS ONE. THAT GUY GETS REALLY DRUNK AND IS SICK ON HER DOG. IT'S GOOD.
OOOH, THAT **DOES** SOUND GOOD!
FINALLY! TODAY IS LOOKING UP!

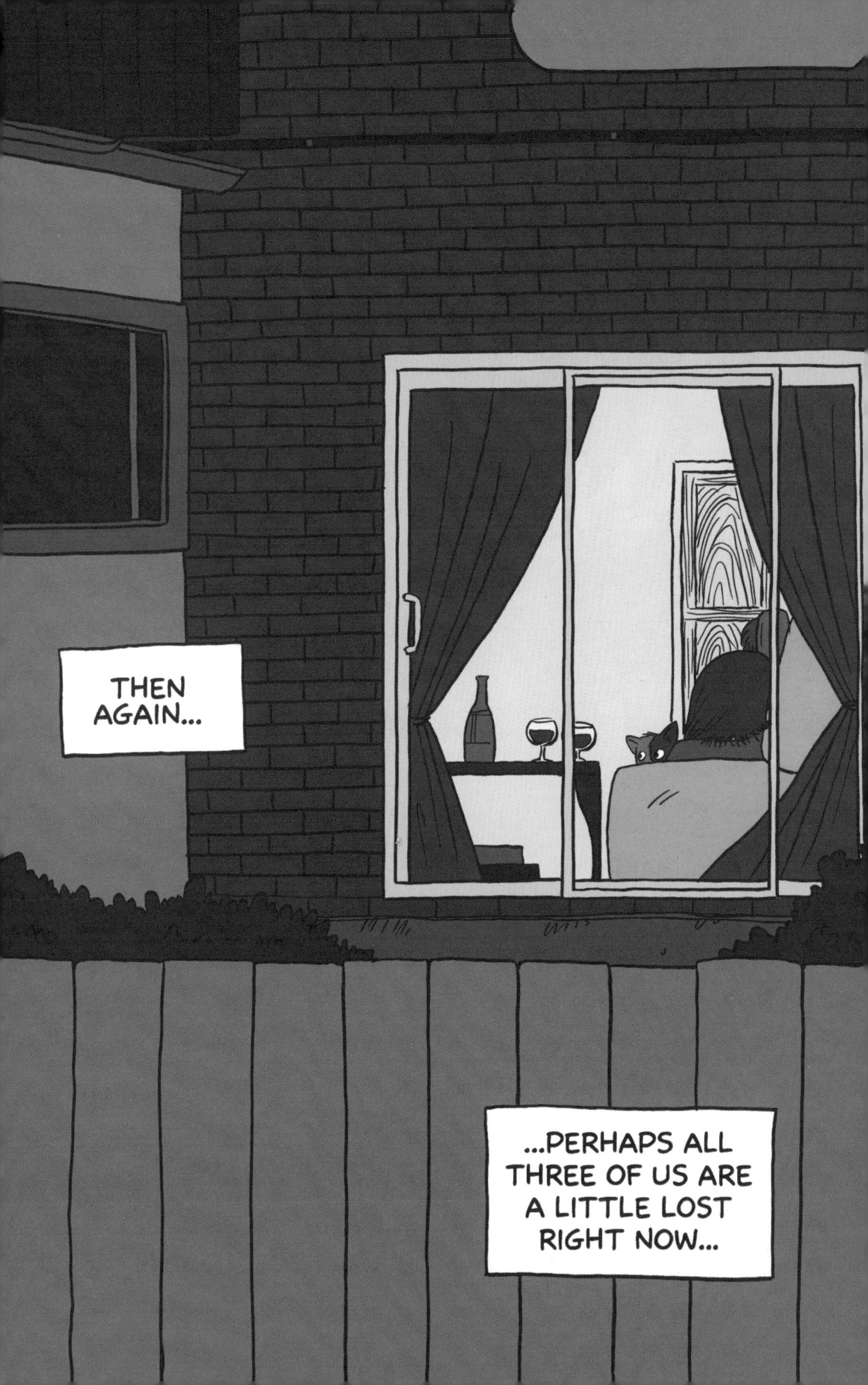
THEN AGAIN...
...PERHAPS ALL THREE OF US ARE A LITTLE LOST RIGHT NOW...

CHAPTER ONE

ILLUSION

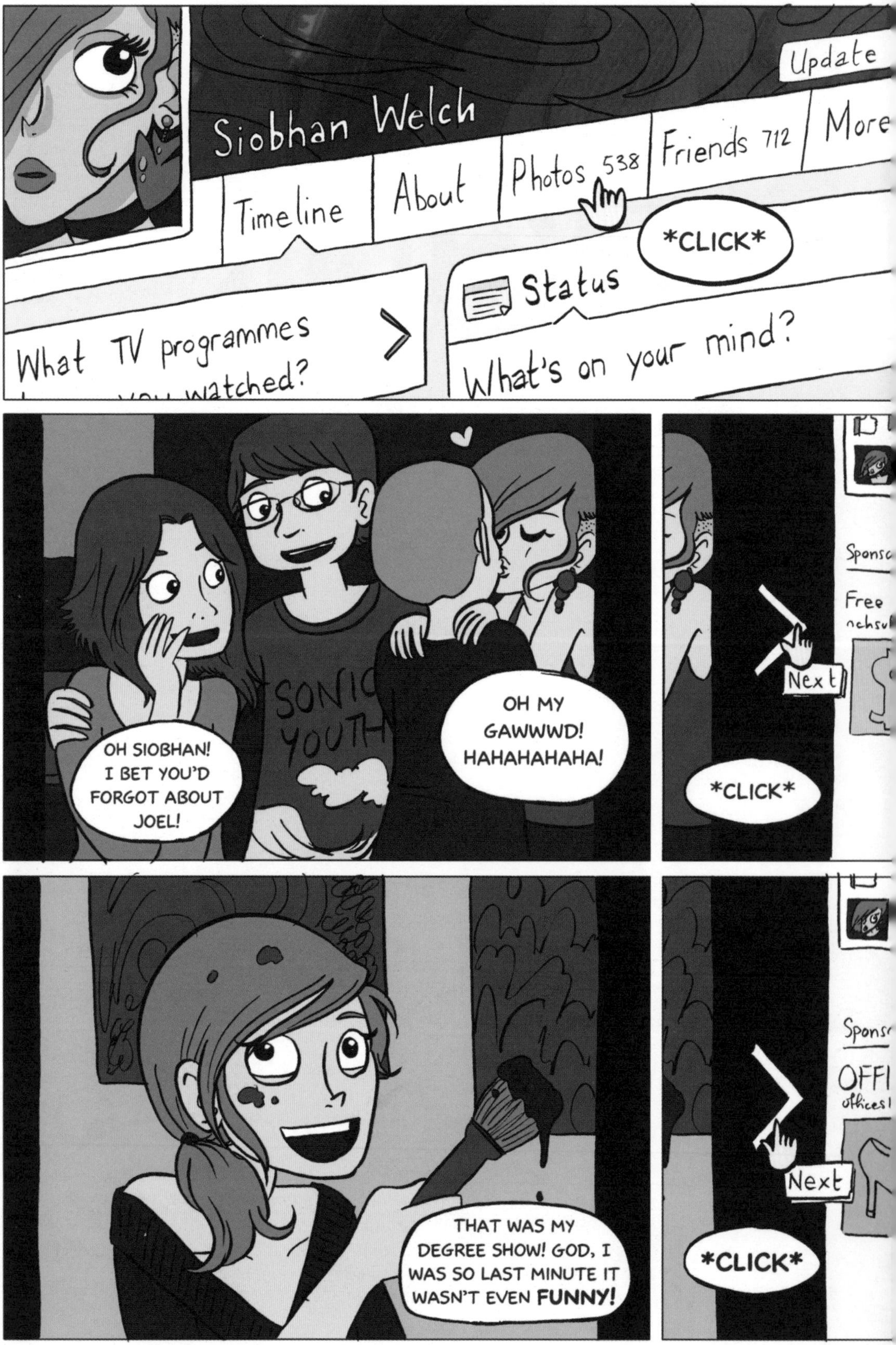
Update
Siobhan Welch
Timeline
About
Photos 538
Friends 712
More
CLICK
Status
What TV programmes
you watched?
What's on your mind?
SONIC YOUTH
OH SIOBHAN! I BET YOU'D FORGOT ABOUT JOEL!
OH MY GAWWWD! HAHAHAHAHA!
Next
CLICK
THAT WAS MY DEGREE SHOW! GOD, I WAS SO LAST MINUTE IT WASN'T EVEN **FUNNY**!
Next
CLICK

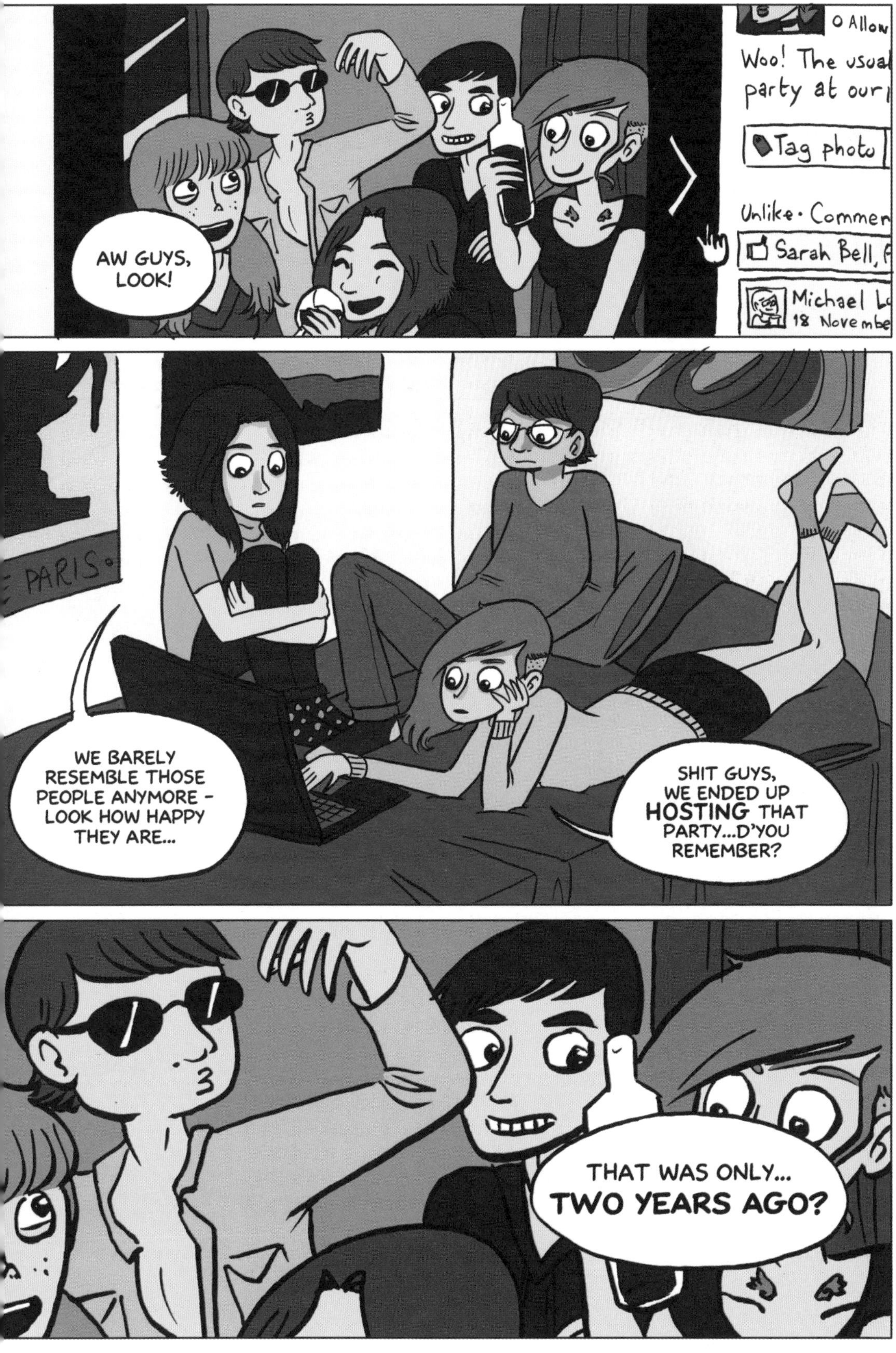

O Allow
Woo! The usua
party at our
Tag photo
Unlike • Commen
Sarah Bell,
Michael L
18 Novembe
AW GUYS, LOOK!
WE BARELY RESEMBLE THOSE PEOPLE ANYMORE - LOOK HOW HAPPY THEY ARE...
SHIT GUYS, WE ENDED UP HOSTING THAT PARTY...D'YOU REMEMBER?
THAT WAS ONLY... TWO YEARS AGO?

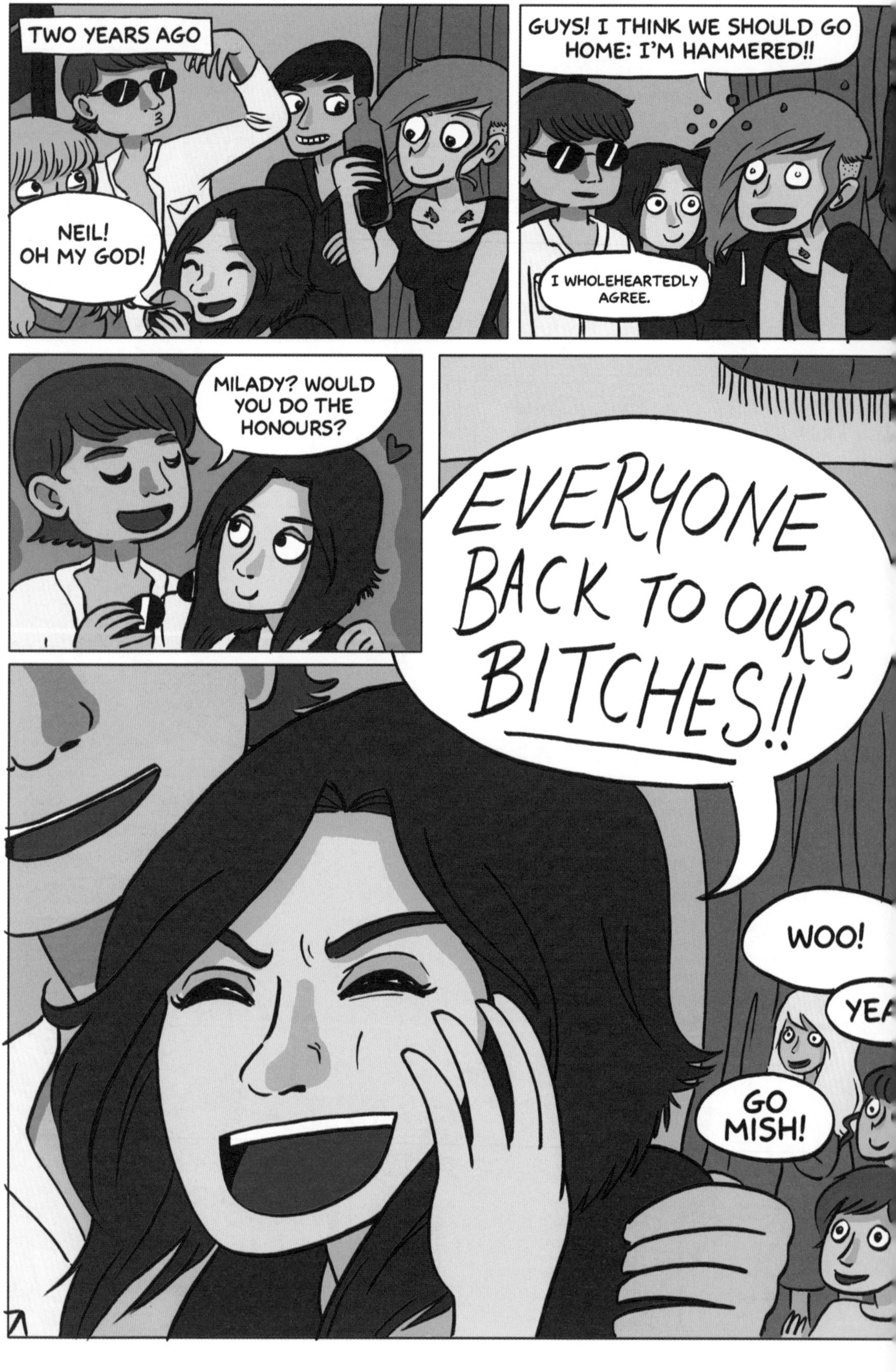
TWO YEARS AGO
NEIL! OH MY GOD!
GUYS! I THINK WE SHOULD GO HOME: I'M HAMMERED!!
I WHOLEHEARTEDLY AGREE.
MILADY? WOULD YOU DO THE HONOURS?
EVERYONE BACK TO OURS, BITCHES!!
WOO!
GO MISH!

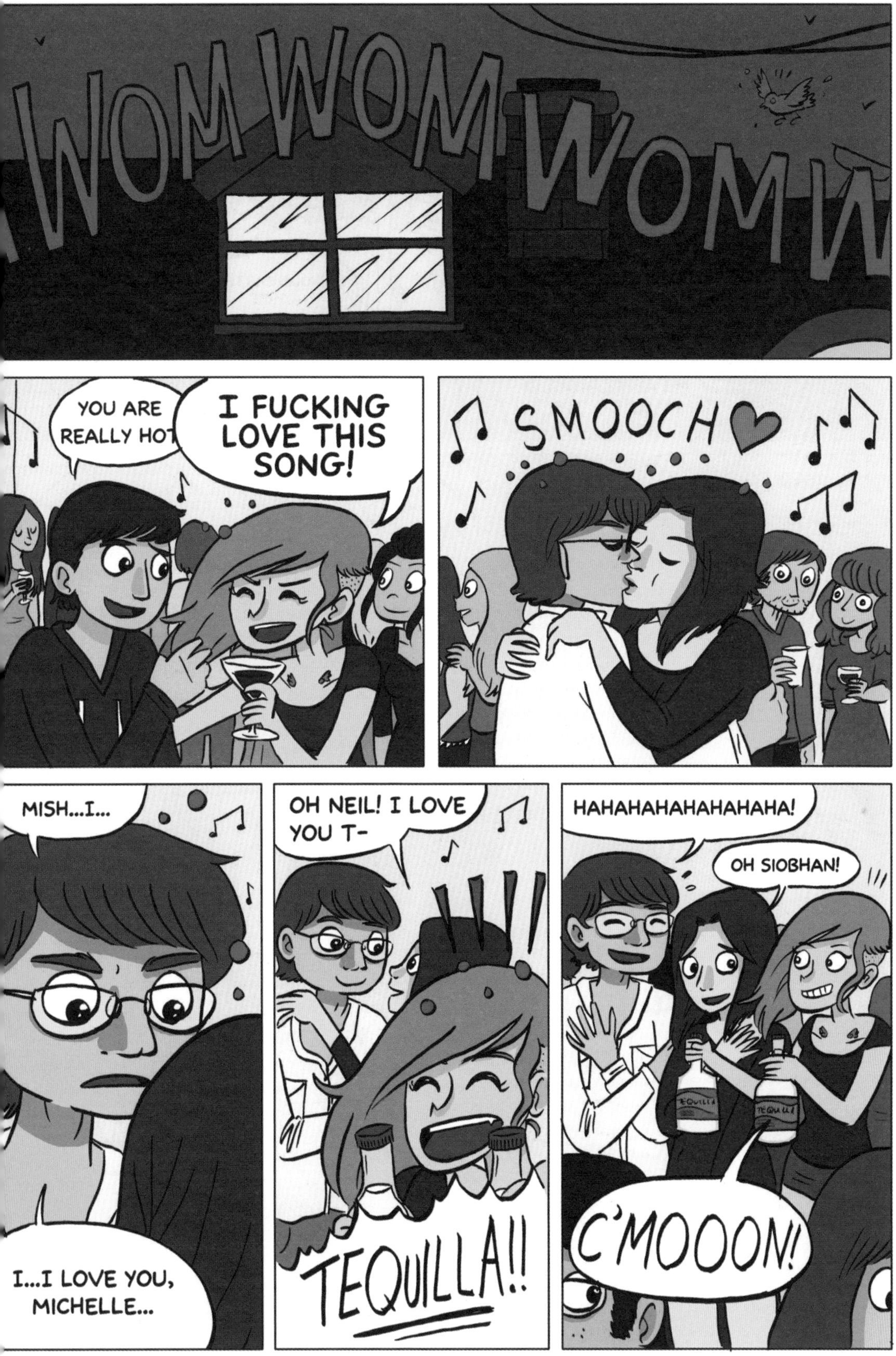
WOMWOMWOMW
YOU ARE REALLY HOT
I FUCKING LOVE THIS SONG!
SMOOCH
MISH...I...
I...I LOVE YOU, MICHELLE...
OH NEIL! I LOVE YOU T-
TEQUILLA!!
HAHAHAHAHAHAHAHA!
OH SIOBHAN!
C'MOOON!

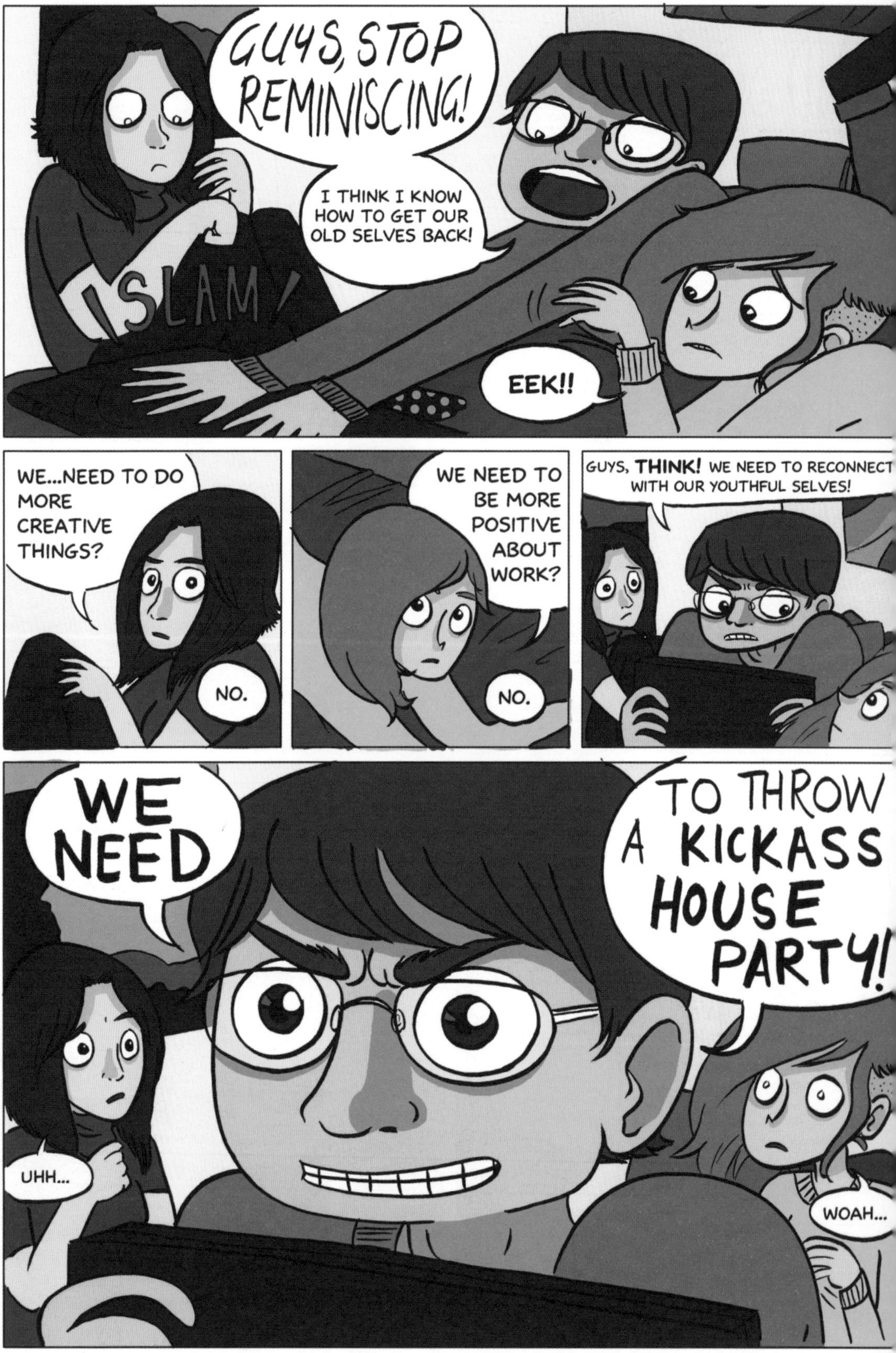
GUYS, STOP REMINISCING!
I THINK I KNOW HOW TO GET OUR OLD SELVES BACK!
SLAM!
EEK!!
WE...NEED TO DO MORE CREATIVE THINGS?
NO.
WE NEED TO BE MORE POSITIVE ABOUT WORK?
NO.
GUYS, THINK! WE NEED TO RECONNECT WITH OUR YOUTHFUL SELVES!
WE NEED
TO THROW A KICKASS HOUSE PARTY!
UHH...
WOAH...

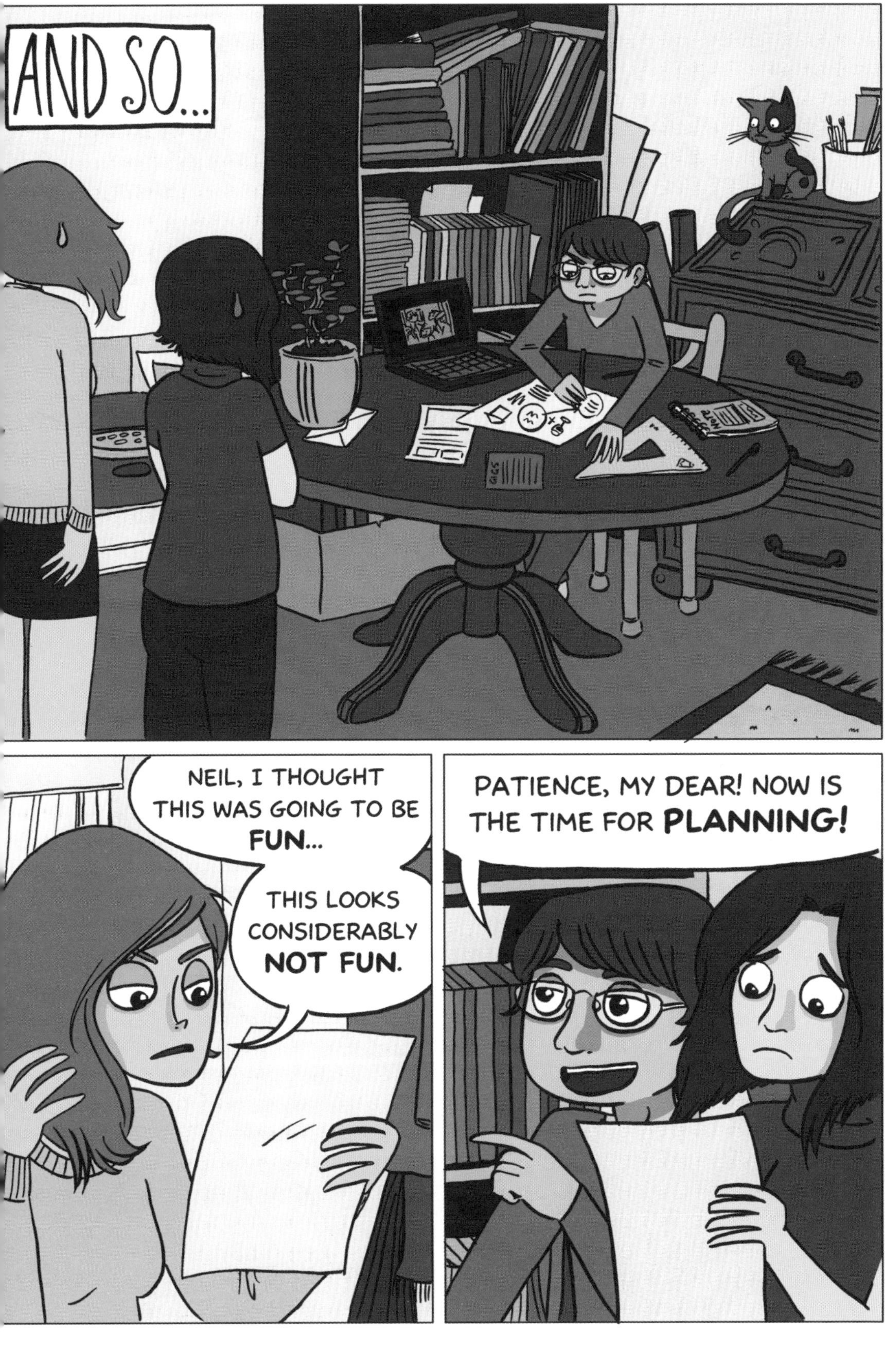
AND SO...
NEIL, I THOUGHT THIS WAS GOING TO BE **FUN**...
THIS LOOKS CONSIDERABLY **NOT FUN**.
PATIENCE, MY DEAR! NOW IS THE TIME FOR **PLANNING**!

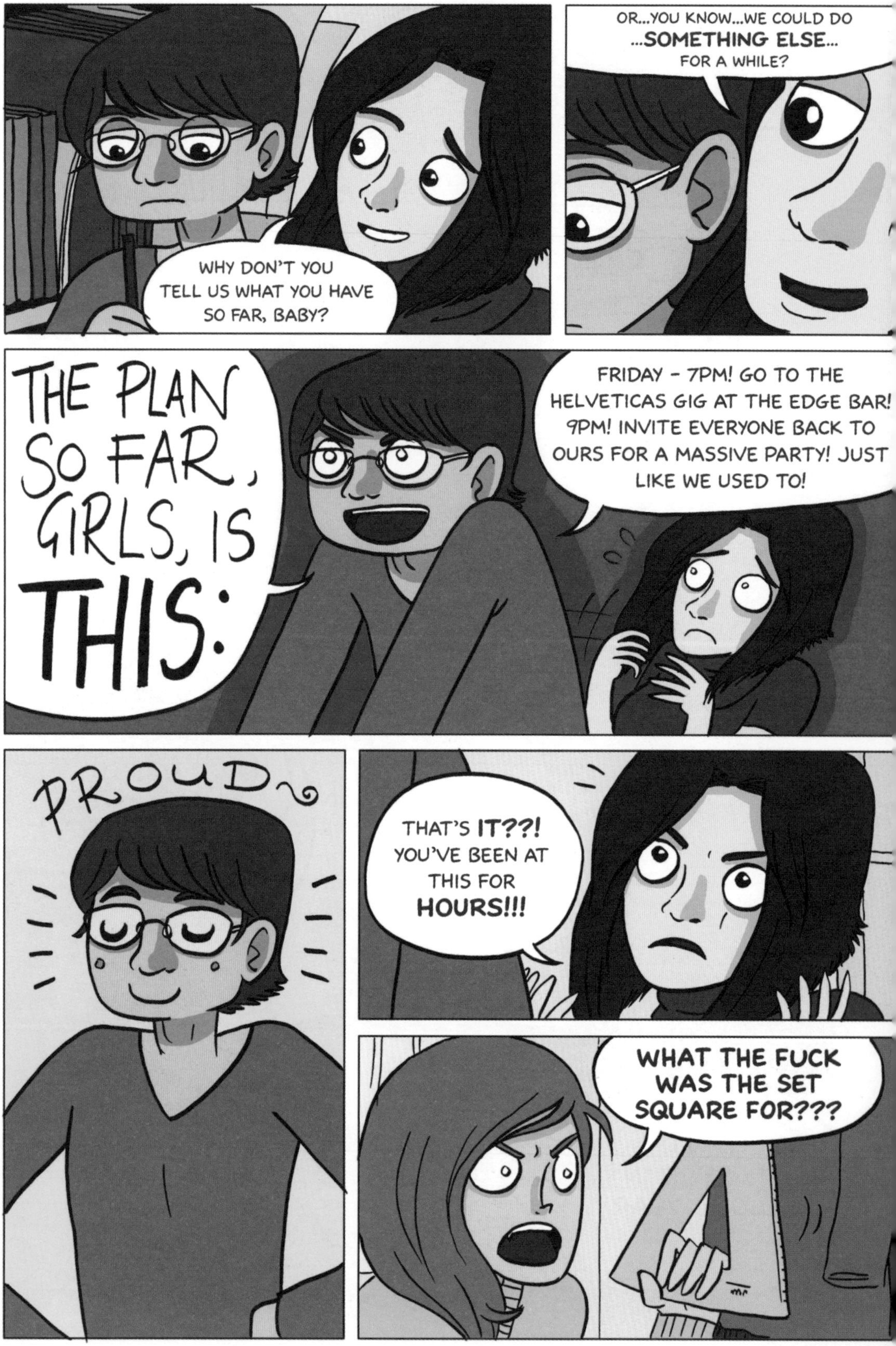
WHY DON'T YOU TELL US WHAT YOU HAVE SO FAR, BABY?
OR...YOU KNOW...WE COULD DO ...SOMETHING ELSE... FOR A WHILE?
THE PLAN SO FAR, GIRLS, IS THIS:
FRIDAY - 7PM! GO TO THE HELVETICAS GIG AT THE EDGE BAR! 9PM! INVITE EVERYONE BACK TO OURS FOR A MASSIVE PARTY! JUST LIKE WE USED TO!
PROUD
THAT'S IT??! YOU'VE BEEN AT THIS FOR HOURS!!!
WHAT THE FUCK WAS THE SET SQUARE FOR???

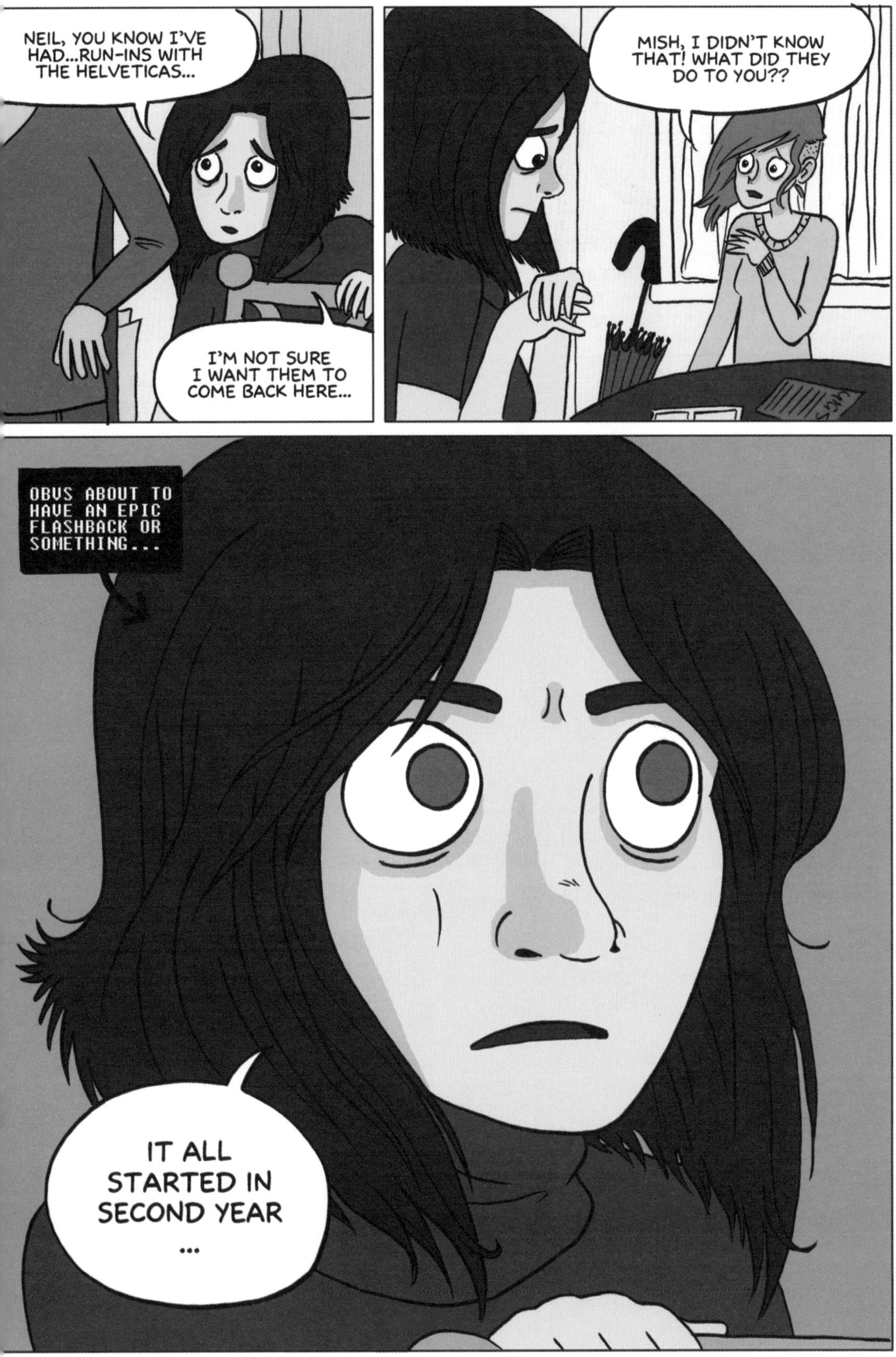
NEIL, YOU KNOW I'VE HAD...RUN-INS WITH THE HELVETICAS...
I'M NOT SURE I WANT THEM TO COME BACK HERE...
MISH, I DIDN'T KNOW THAT! WHAT DID THEY DO TO YOU??
OBVS ABOUT TO HAVE AN EPIC FLASHBACK OR SOMETHING...
IT ALL STARTED IN SECOND YEAR ...

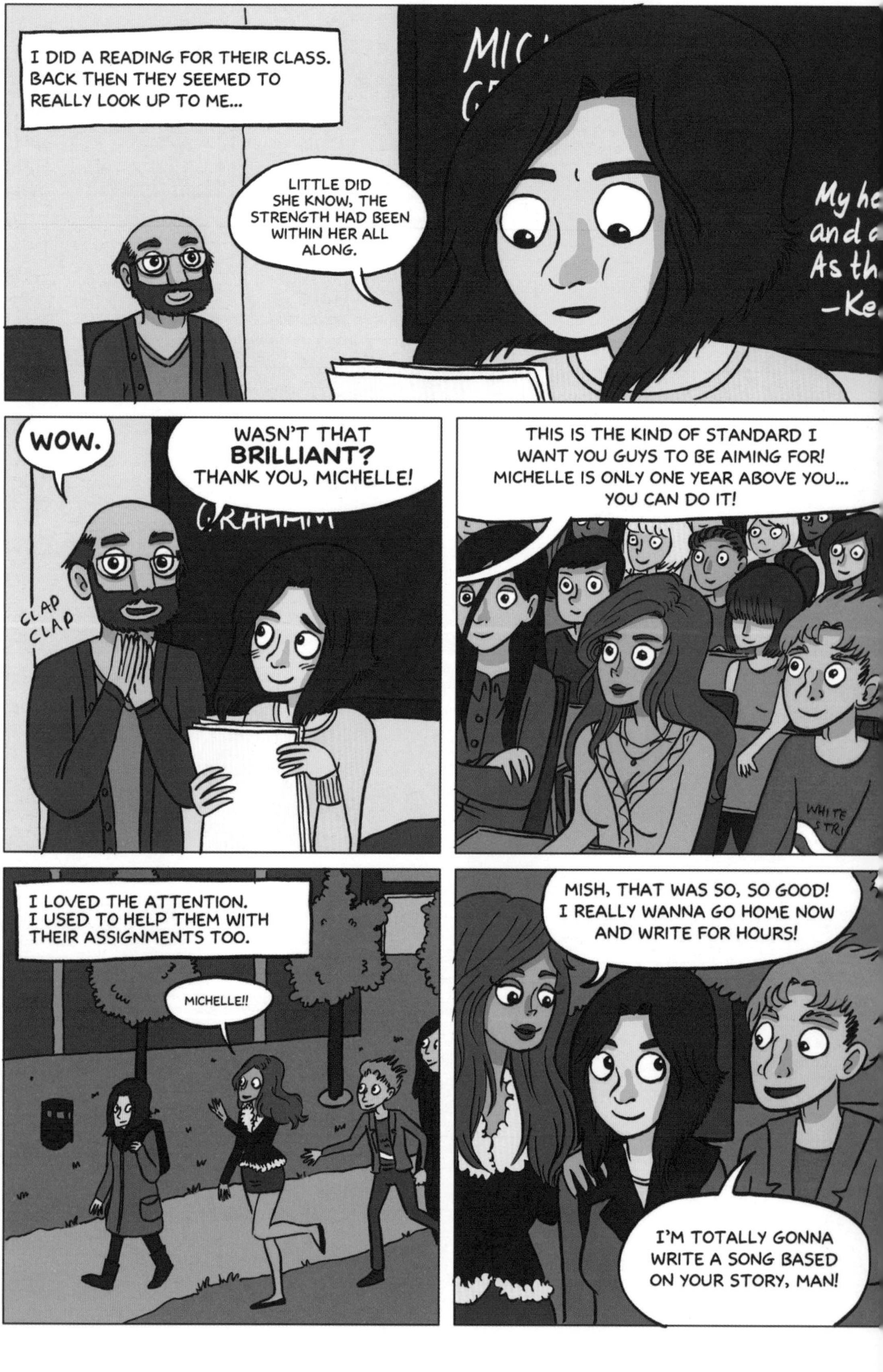
I DID A READING FOR THEIR CLASS. BACK THEN THEY SEEMED TO REALLY LOOK UP TO ME...
LITTLE DID SHE KNOW, THE STRENGTH HAD BEEN WITHIN HER ALL ALONG.
WOW.
WASN'T THAT **BRILLIANT?** THANK YOU, MICHELLE!
CLAP CLAP
THIS IS THE KIND OF STANDARD I WANT YOU GUYS TO BE AIMING FOR! MICHELLE IS ONLY ONE YEAR ABOVE YOU... YOU CAN DO IT!
I LOVED THE ATTENTION. I USED TO HELP THEM WITH THEIR ASSIGNMENTS TOO.
MICHELLE!!
MISH, THAT WAS SO, SO GOOD! I REALLY WANNA GO HOME NOW AND WRITE FOR HOURS!
I'M TOTALLY GONNA WRITE A SONG BASED ON YOUR STORY, MAN!

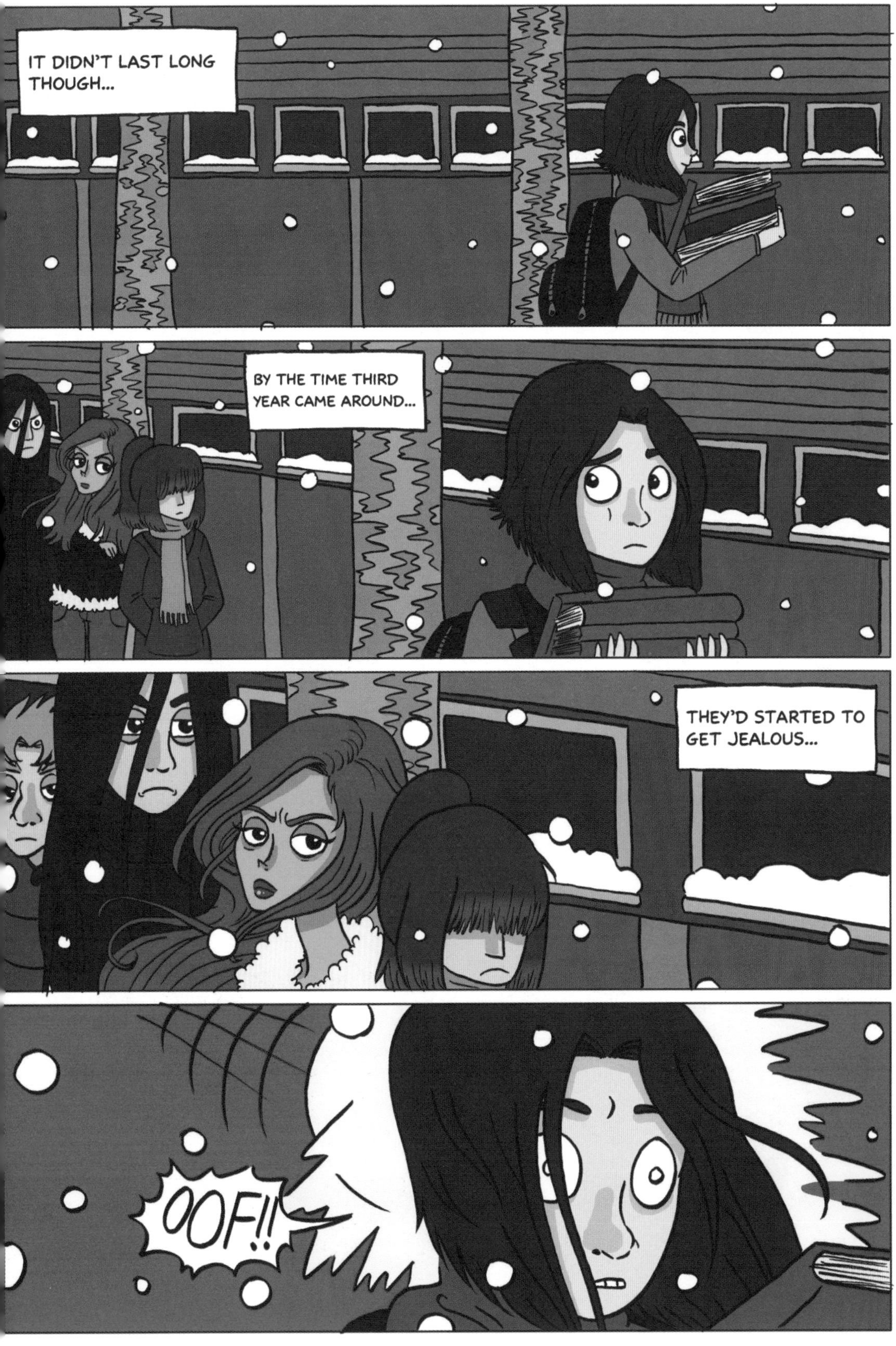
IT DIDN'T LAST LONG THOUGH...
BY THE TIME THIRD YEAR CAME AROUND...
THEY'D STARTED TO GET JEALOUS...
OOF!!

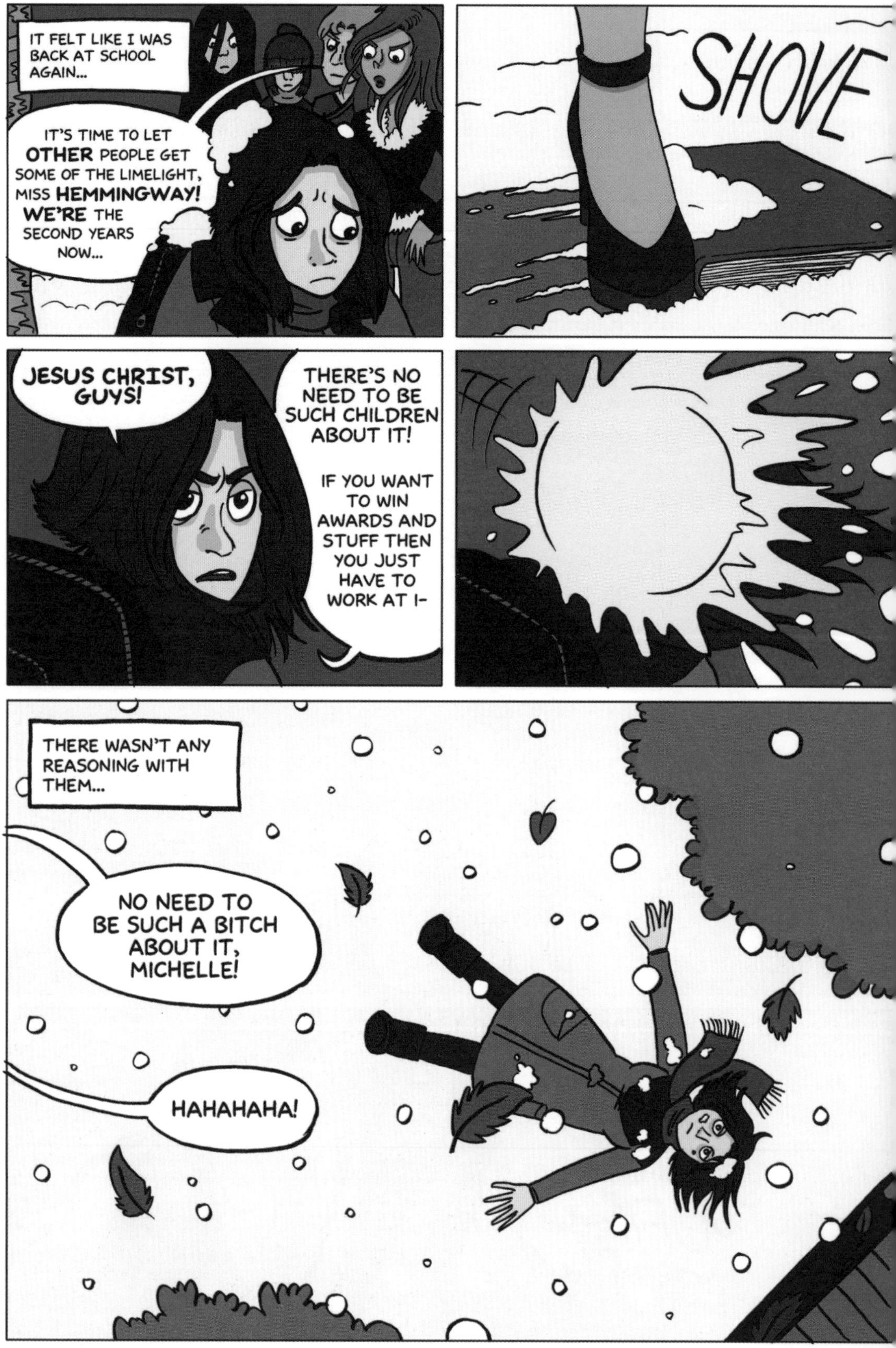
IT FELT LIKE I WAS BACK AT SCHOOL AGAIN...
IT'S TIME TO LET OTHER PEOPLE GET SOME OF THE LIMELIGHT, MISS HEMMINGWAY! WE'RE THE SECOND YEARS NOW...
SHOVE
JESUS CHRIST, GUYS!
THERE'S NO NEED TO BE SUCH CHILDREN ABOUT IT!
IF YOU WANT TO WIN AWARDS AND STUFF THEN YOU JUST HAVE TO WORK AT I-
THERE WASN'T ANY REASONING WITH THEM...
NO NEED TO BE SUCH A BITCH ABOUT IT, MICHELLE!
HAHAHAHA!

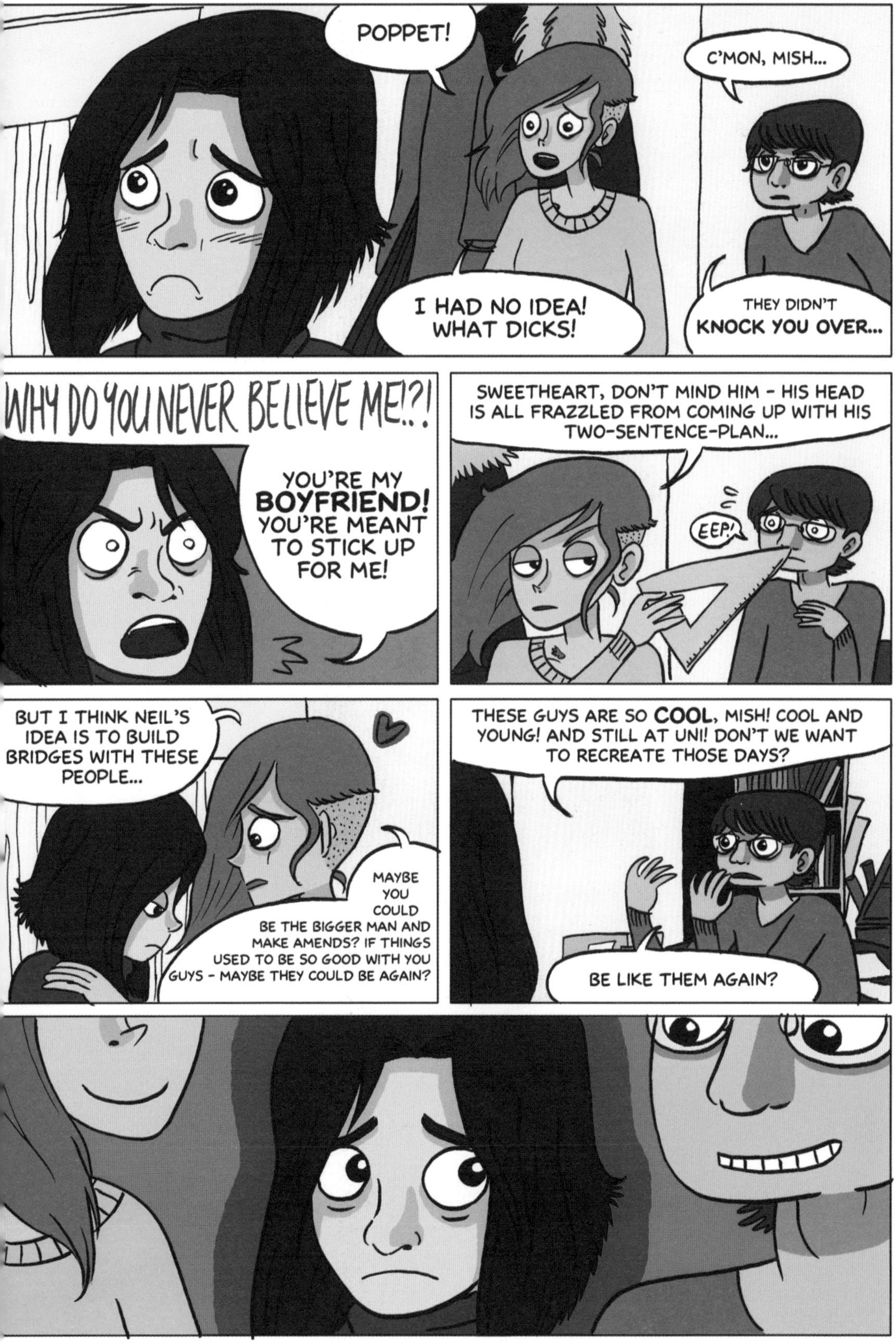

POPPET!
C'MON, MISH...
I HAD NO IDEA! WHAT DICKS!
THEY DIDN'T KNOCK YOU OVER...
WHY DO YOU NEVER BELIEVE ME!?!
YOU'RE MY BOYFRIEND! YOU'RE MEANT TO STICK UP FOR ME!
SWEETHEART, DON'T MIND HIM - HIS HEAD IS ALL FRAZZLED FROM COMING UP WITH HIS TWO-SENTENCE-PLAN...
EEP!
BUT I THINK NEIL'S IDEA IS TO BUILD BRIDGES WITH THESE PEOPLE...
MAYBE YOU COULD BE THE BIGGER MAN AND MAKE AMENDS? IF THINGS USED TO BE SO GOOD WITH YOU GUYS - MAYBE THEY COULD BE AGAIN?
THESE GUYS ARE SO COOL, MISH! COOL AND YOUNG! AND STILL AT UNI! DON'T WE WANT TO RECREATE THOSE DAYS?
BE LIKE THEM AGAIN?

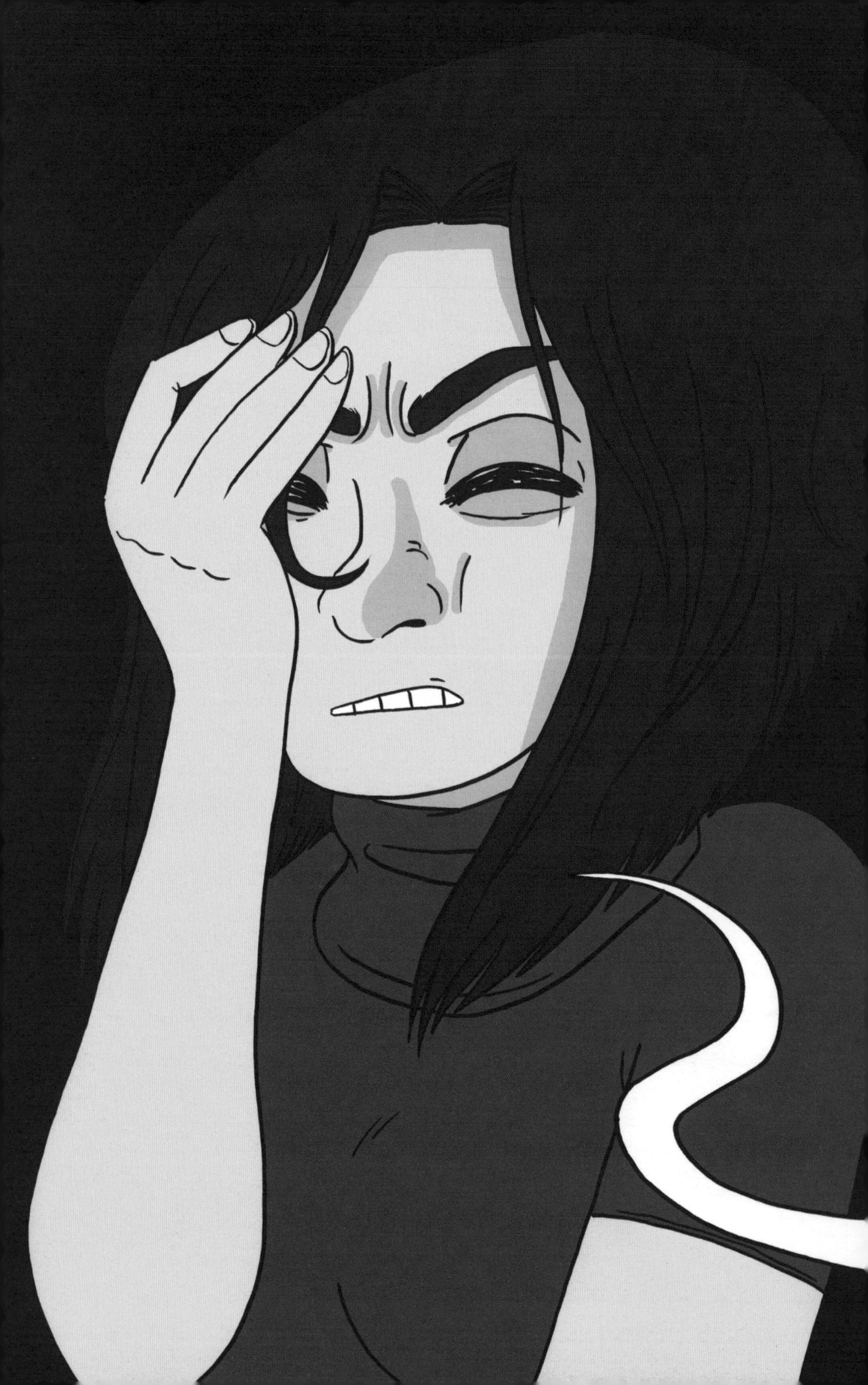

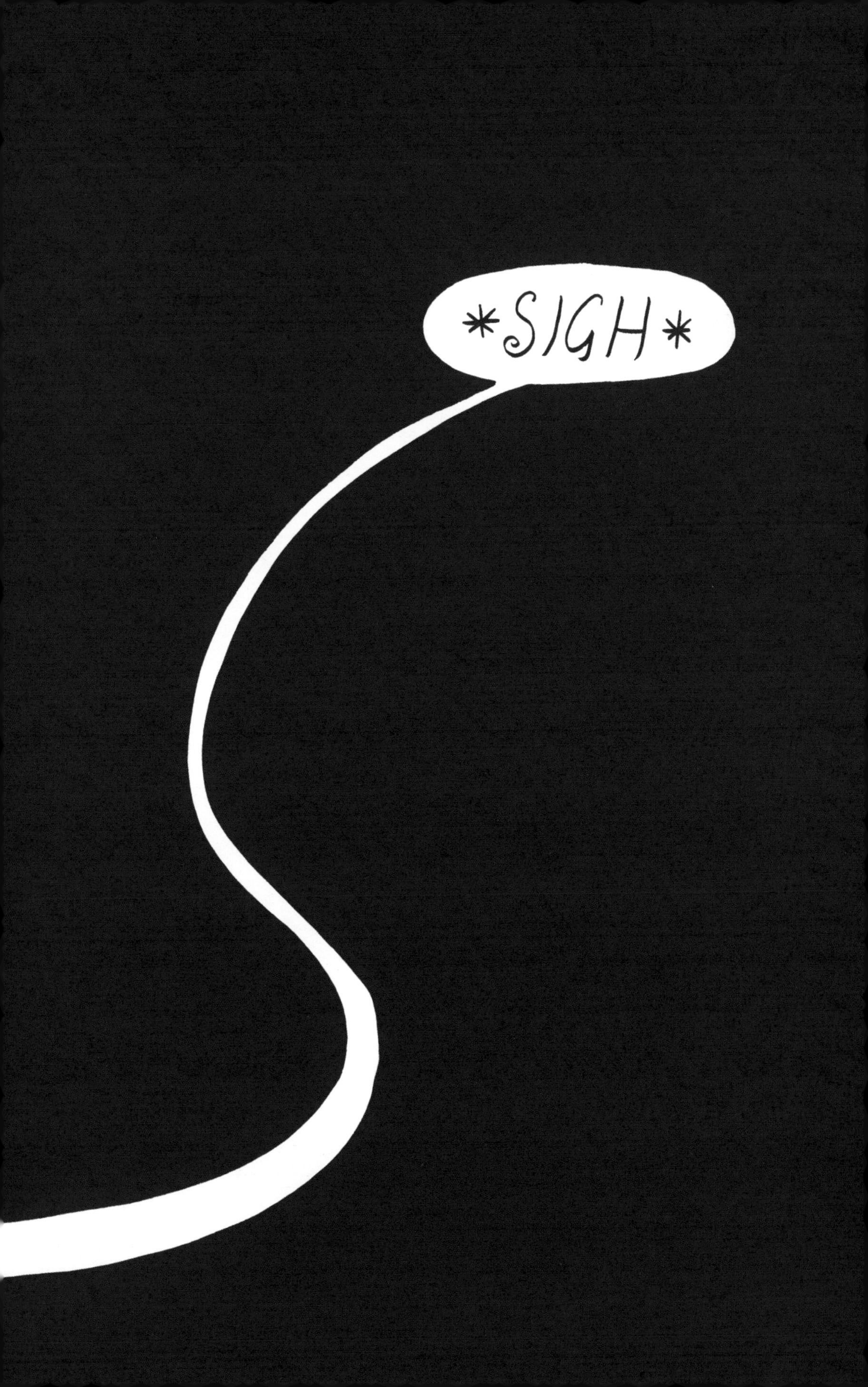
SIGH

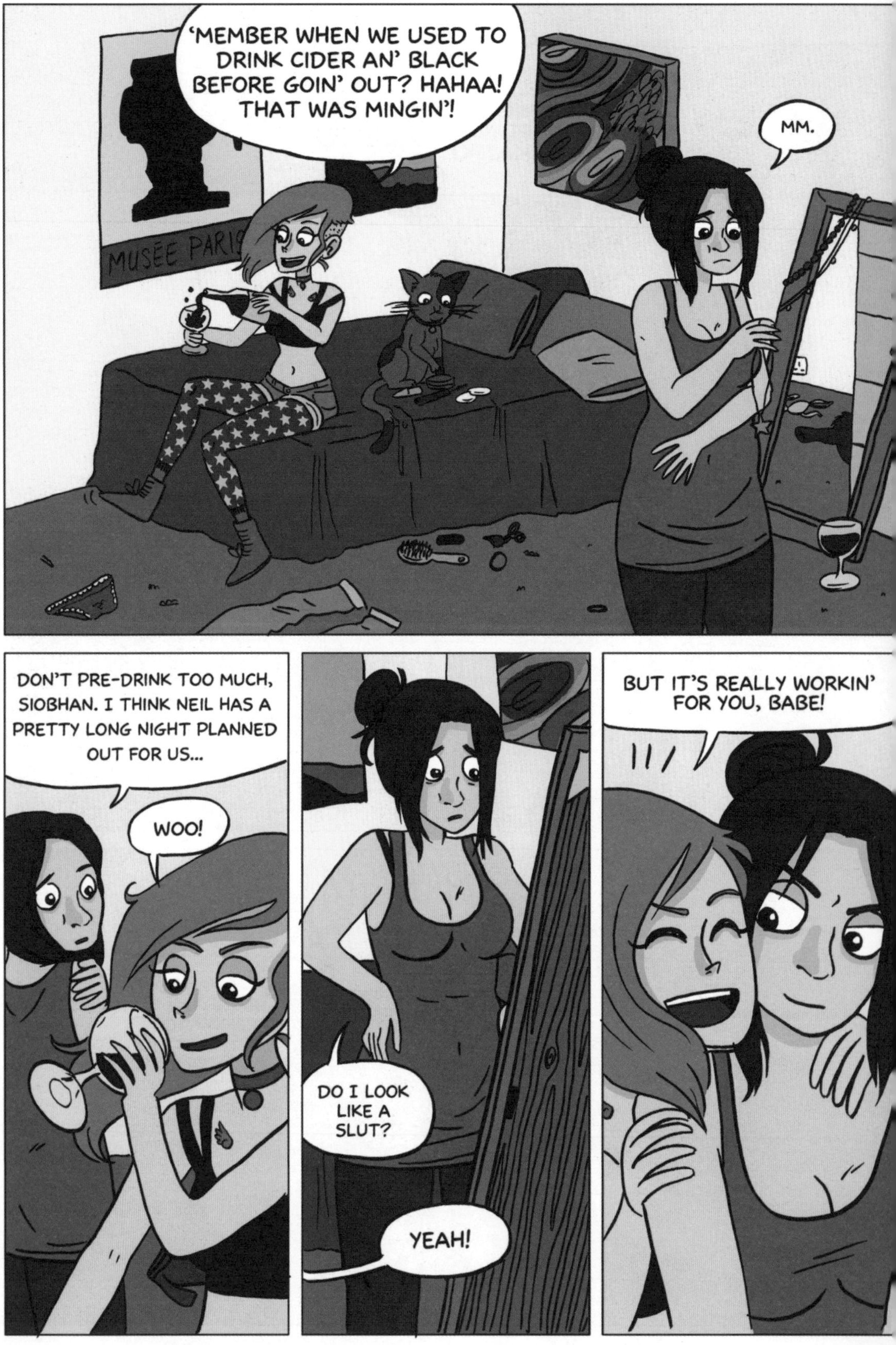

'MEMBER WHEN WE USED TO DRINK CIDER AN' BLACK BEFORE GOIN' OUT? HAHAA! THAT WAS MINGIN'!
MUSEE PARIS
MM.
DON'T PRE-DRINK TOO MUCH, SIOBHAN. I THINK NEIL HAS A PRETTY LONG NIGHT PLANNED OUT FOR US...
WOO!
DO I LOOK LIKE A SLUT?
YEAH!
BUT IT'S REALLY WORKIN' FOR YOU, BABE!

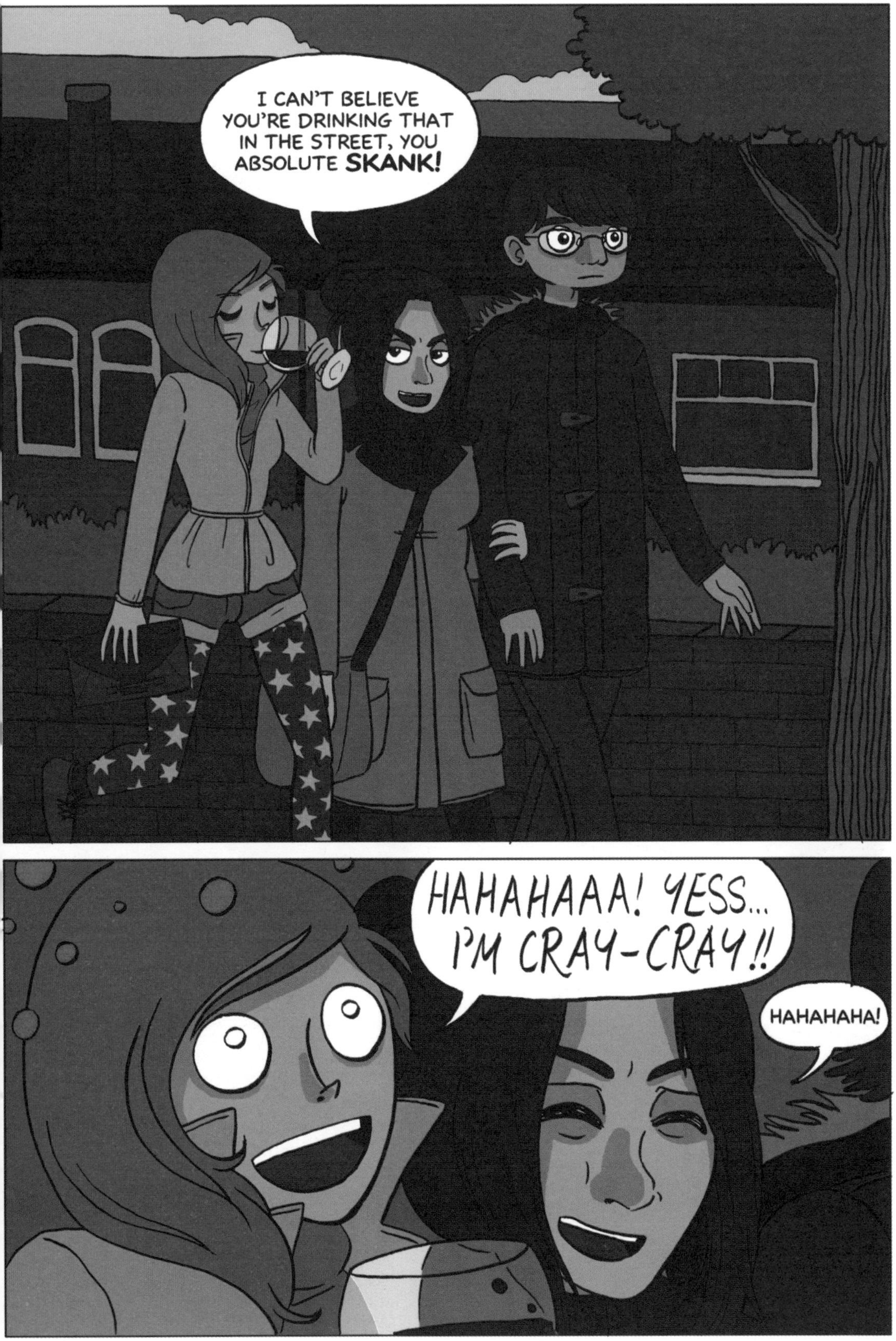
I CAN'T BELIEVE YOU'RE DRINKING THAT IN THE STREET, YOU ABSOLUTE SKANK!
HAHAHAAA! YESS... I'M CRAY-CRAY!!
HAHAHAHA!

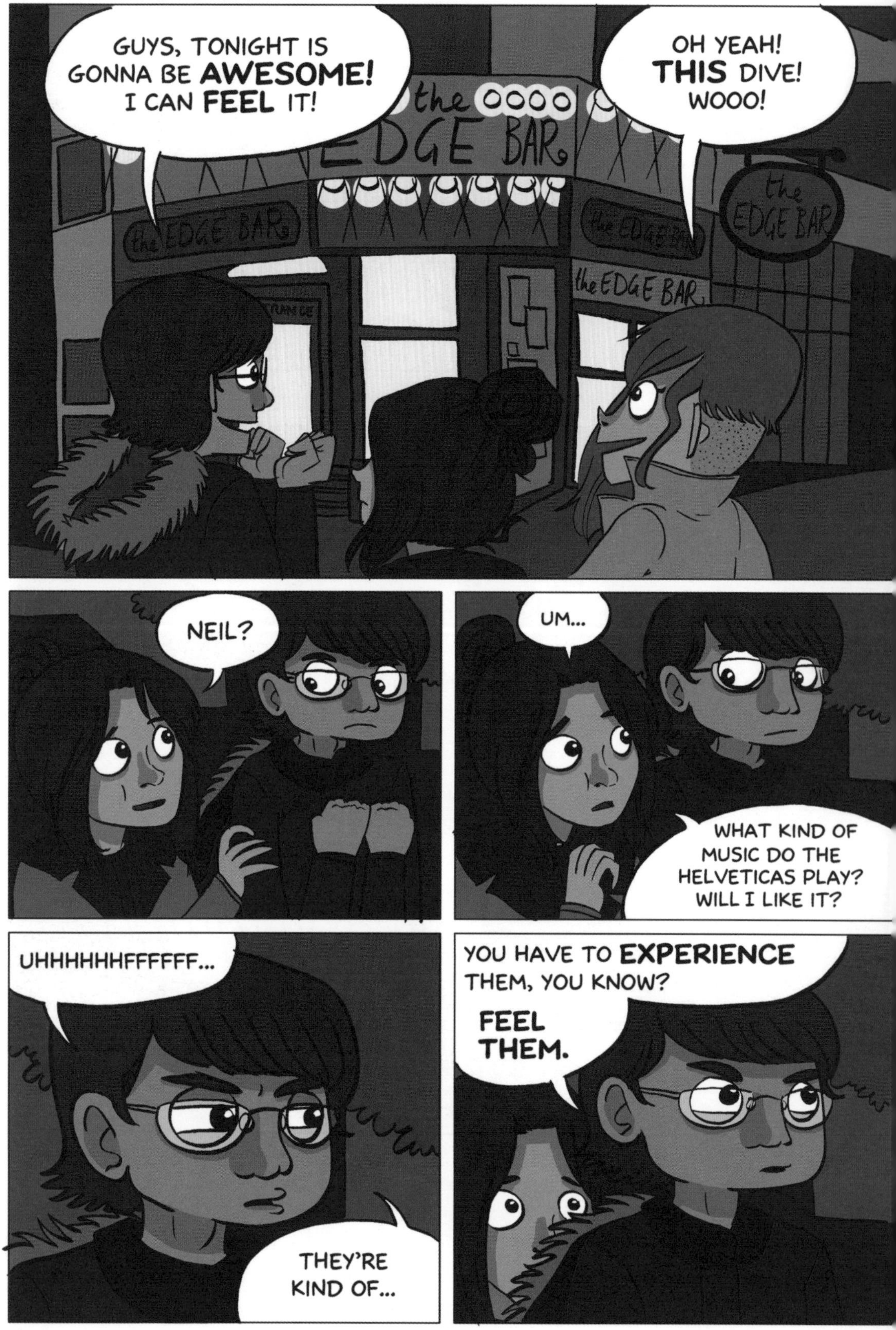
GUYS, TONIGHT IS GONNA BE **AWESOME!** I CAN **FEEL** IT!
OH YEAH! **THIS** DIVE! WOOO!
the EDGE BAR
NEIL?
UM...
WHAT KIND OF MUSIC DO THE HELVETICAS PLAY? WILL I LIKE IT?
UHHHHHHFFFFFF...
THEY'RE KIND OF...
YOU HAVE TO **EXPERIENCE** THEM, YOU KNOW?
FEEL THEM.

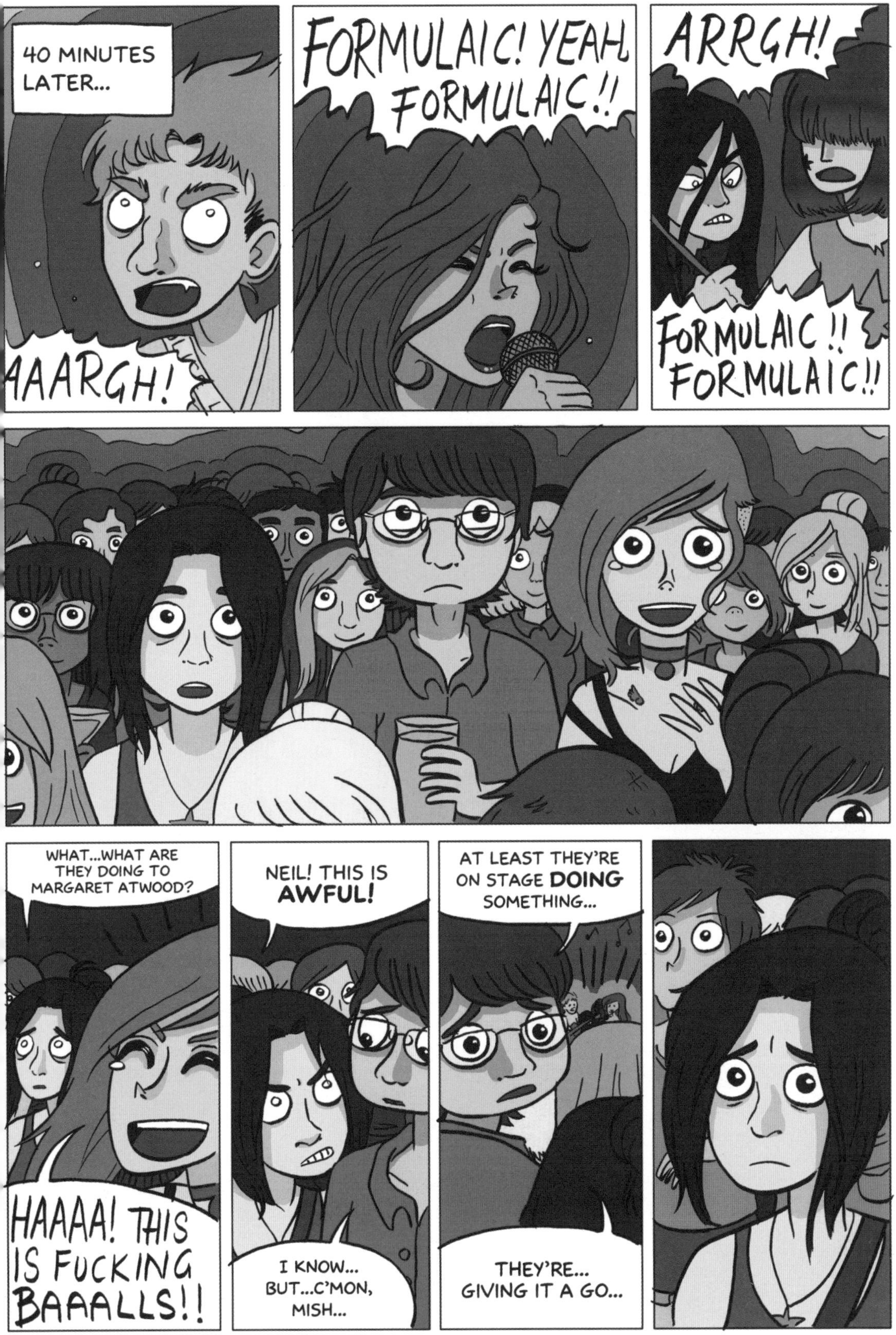

40 MINUTES LATER...
AAARGH!
FORMULAIC! YEAH FORMULAIC!!
ARRGH!
FORMULAIC!! FORMULAIC!!
WHAT...WHAT ARE THEY DOING TO MARGARET ATWOOD?
HAAAA! THIS IS FUCKING BAAALLS!!
NEIL! THIS IS **AWFUL!**
I KNOW... BUT...C'MON, MISH...
AT LEAST THEY'RE ON STAGE **DOING** SOMETHING...
THEY'RE... GIVING IT A GO...

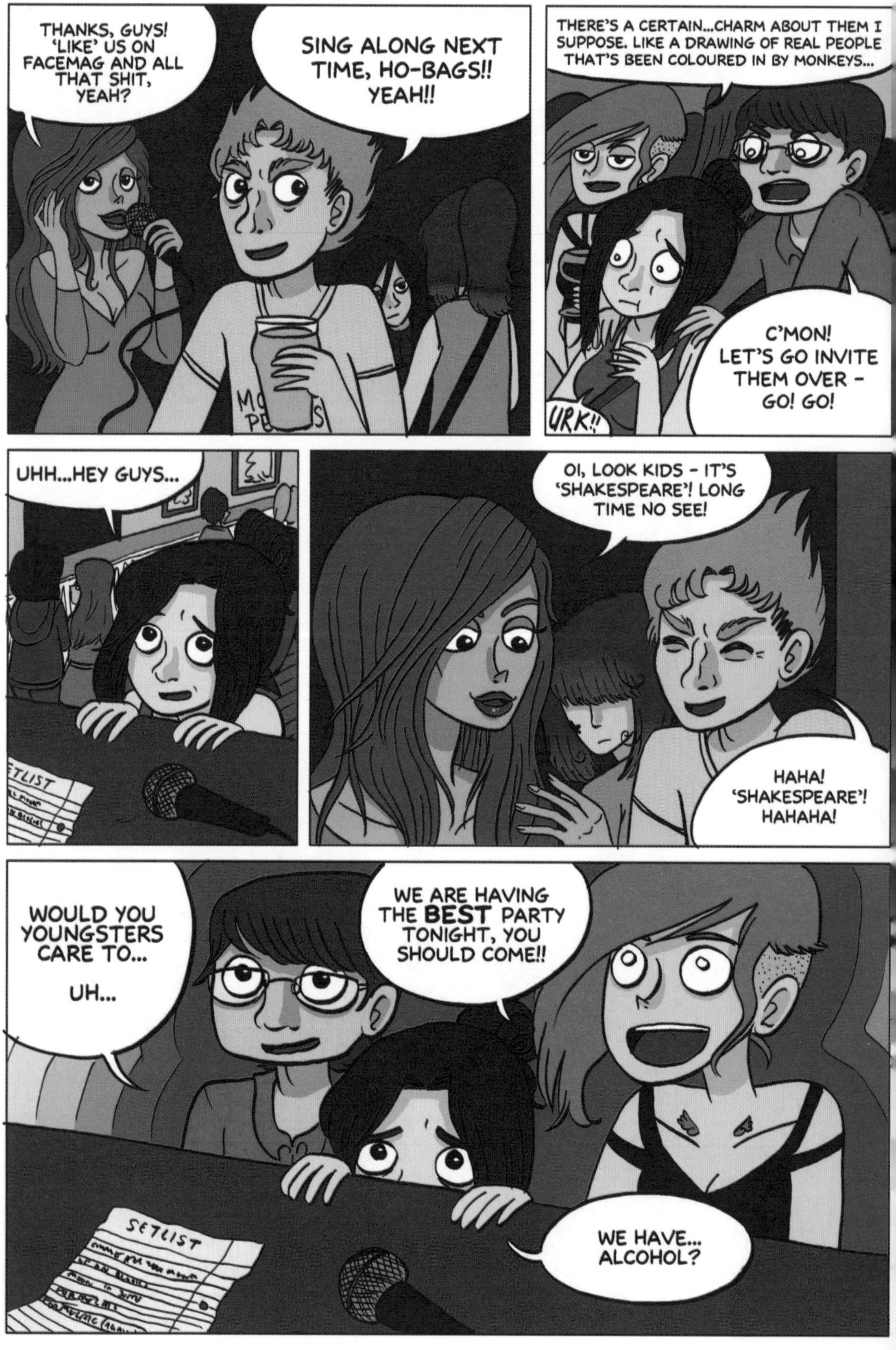
THANKS, GUYS! 'LIKE' US ON FACEMAG AND ALL THAT SHIT, YEAH?
SING ALONG NEXT TIME, HO-BAGS!! YEAH!!
THERE'S A CERTAIN...CHARM ABOUT THEM I SUPPOSE. LIKE A DRAWING OF REAL PEOPLE THAT'S BEEN COLOURED IN BY MONKEYS...
C'MON! LET'S GO INVITE THEM OVER - GO! GO!
URK!!
UHH...HEY GUYS...
SETLIST
OI, LOOK KIDS - IT'S 'SHAKESPEARE'! LONG TIME NO SEE!
HAHA! 'SHAKESPEARE'! HAHAHA!
WOULD YOU YOUNGSTERS CARE TO...
UH...
WE ARE HAVING THE **BEST** PARTY TONIGHT, YOU SHOULD COME!!
SETLIST
WE HAVE... ALCOHOL?

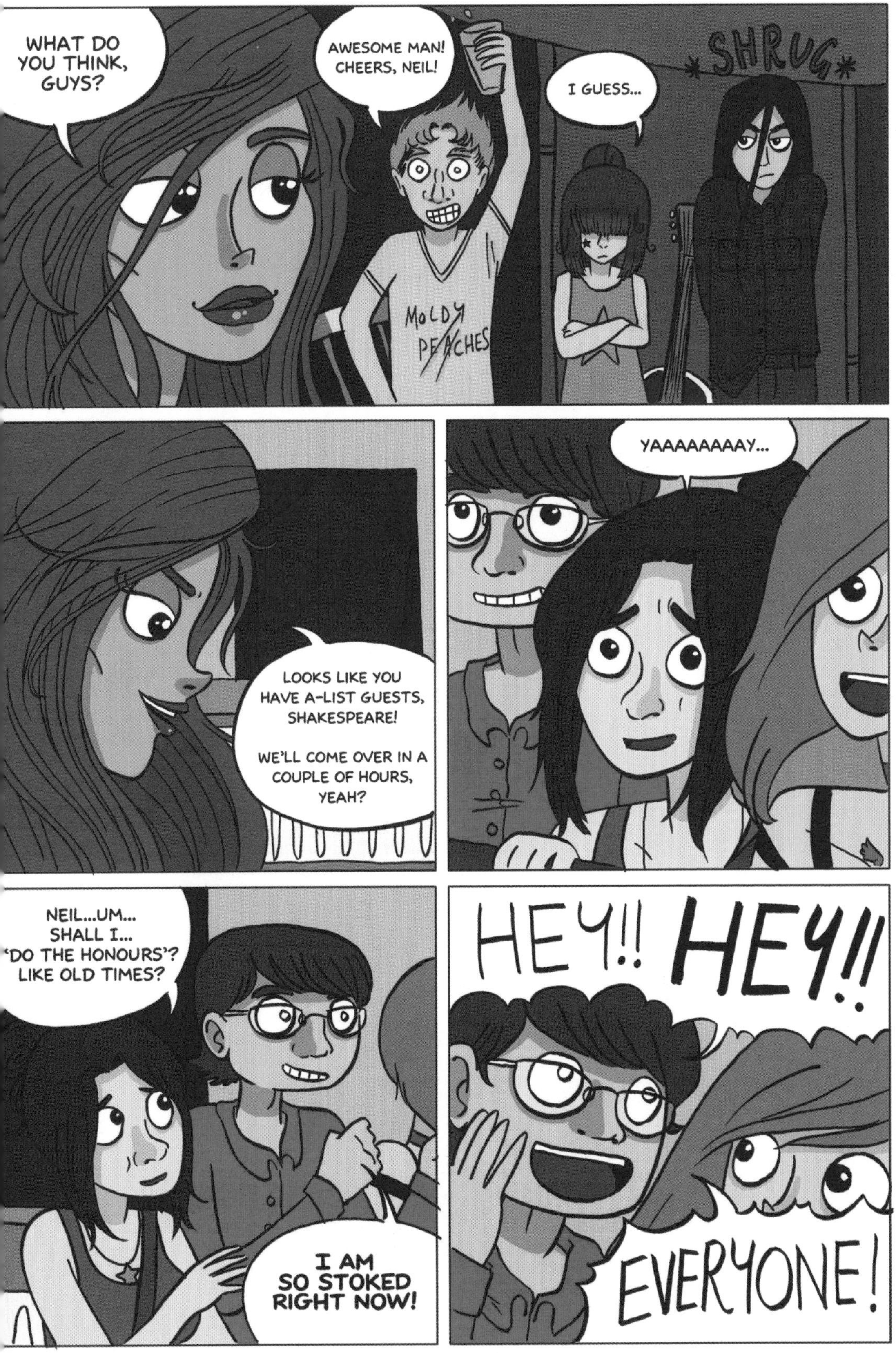
WHAT DO YOU THINK, GUYS?
AWESOME MAN! CHEERS, NEIL!
I GUESS...
SHRUG
MOLDY PEACHES
LOOKS LIKE YOU HAVE A-LIST GUESTS, SHAKESPEARE!
WE'LL COME OVER IN A COUPLE OF HOURS, YEAH?
YAAAAAAAAY...
NEIL...UM... SHALL I... 'DO THE HONOURS'? LIKE OLD TIMES?
I AM SO STOKED RIGHT NOW!
HEY!! HEY!!
EVERYONE!

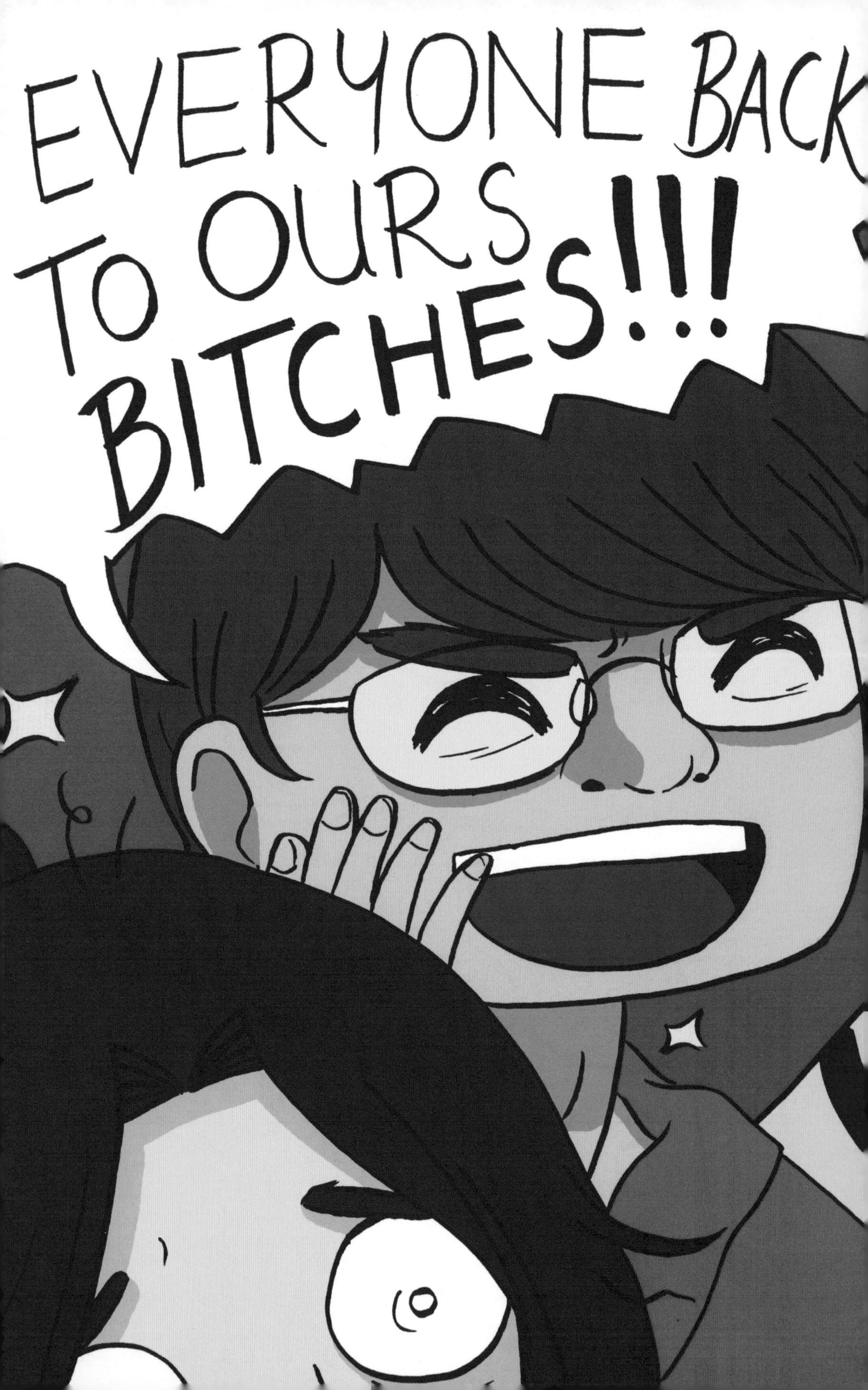
EVERYONE BACK TO OURS BITCHES!!!

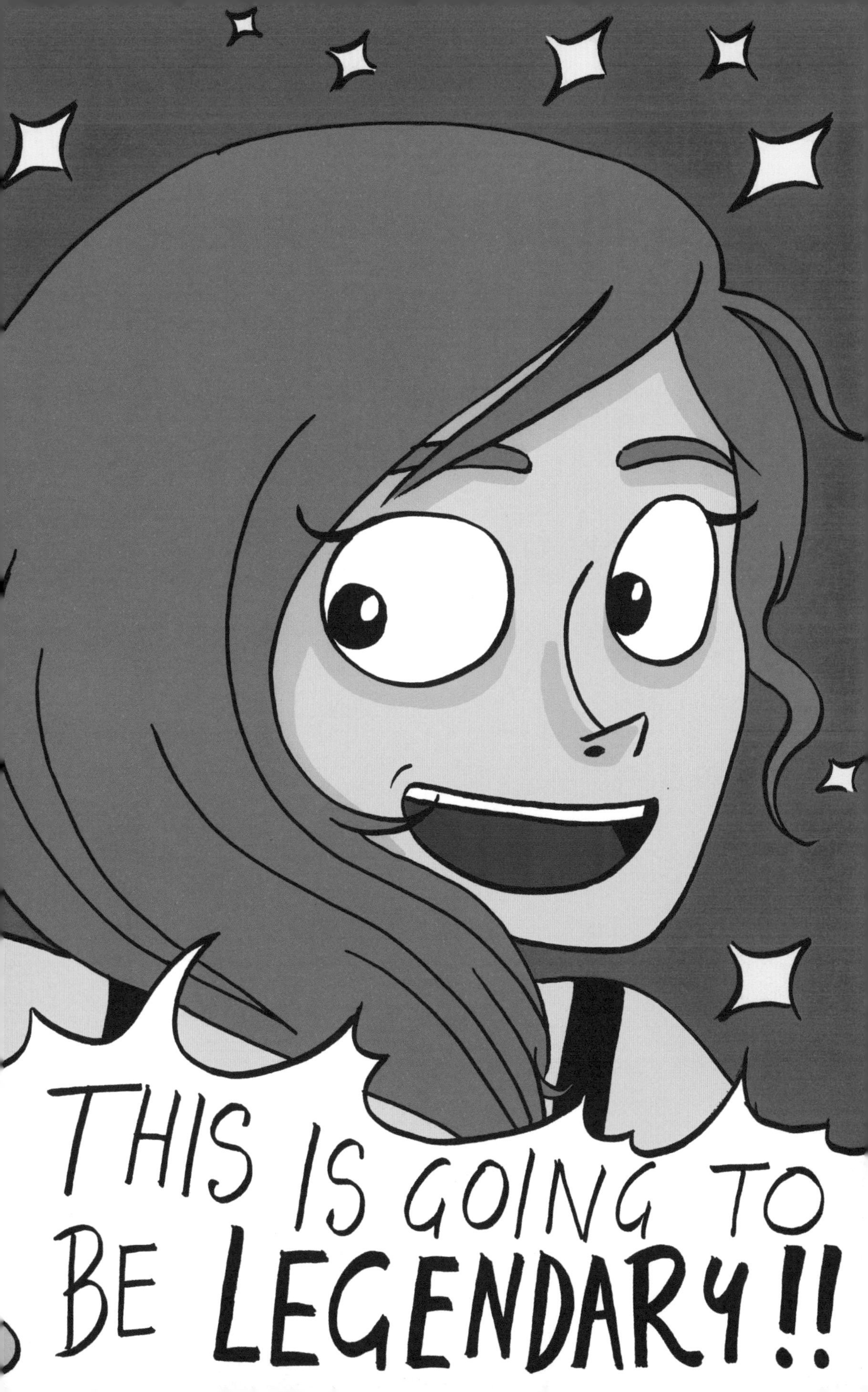
THIS IS GOING TO BE LEGENDARY!!

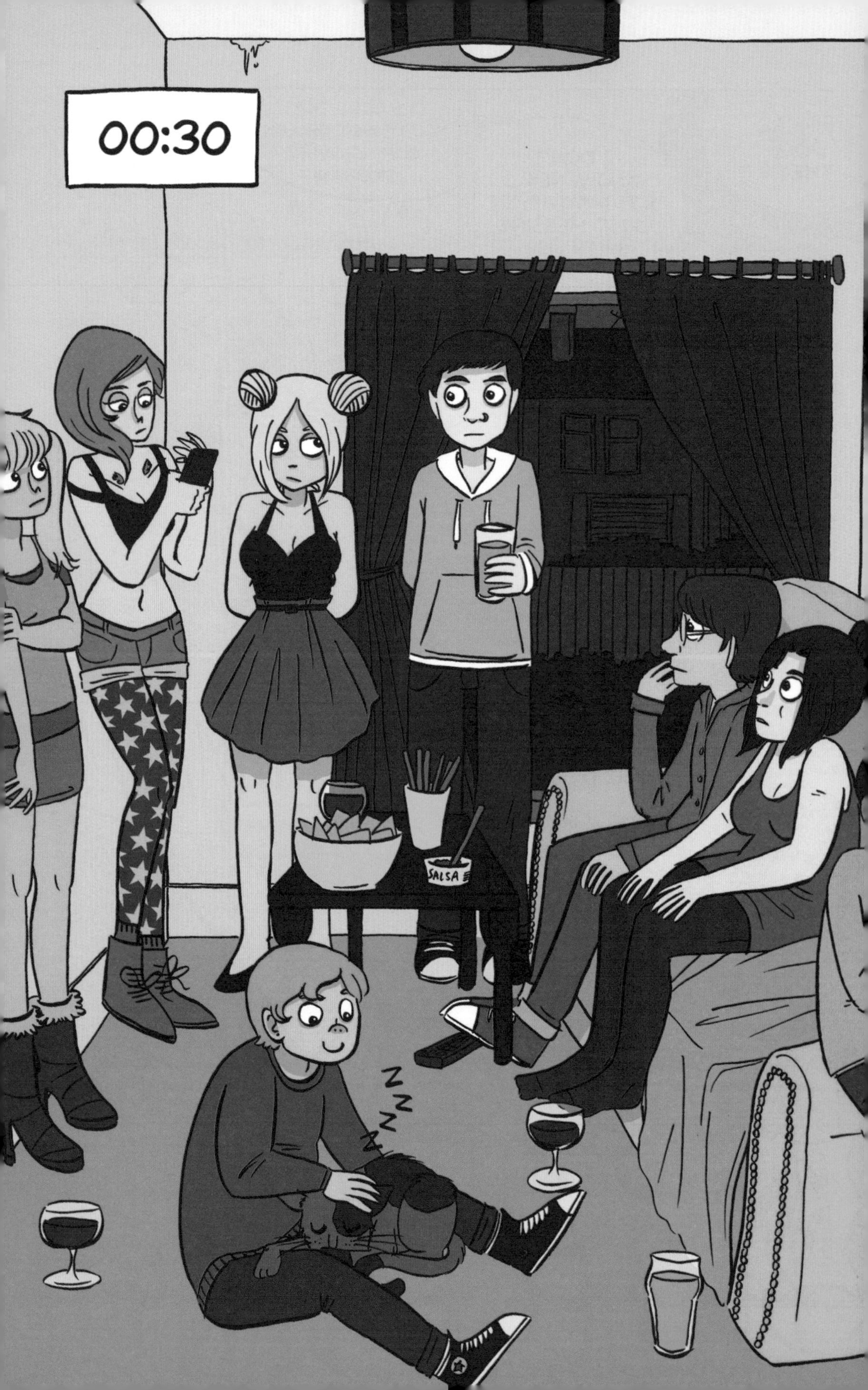
00:30
SALSA
ZZZ

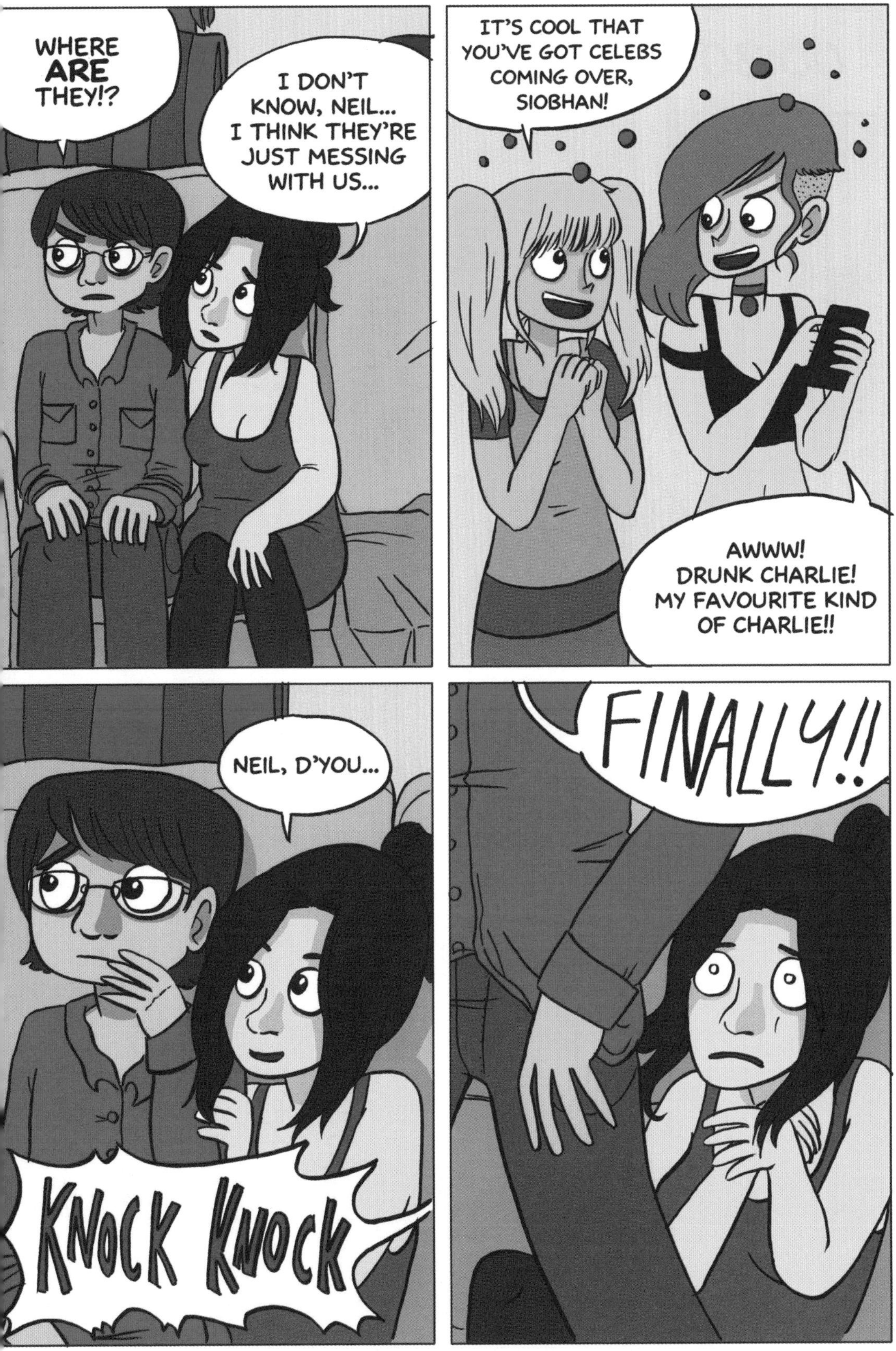
WHERE ARE THEY!?
I DON'T KNOW, NEIL... I THINK THEY'RE JUST MESSING WITH US...
IT'S COOL THAT YOU'VE GOT CELEBS COMING OVER, SIOBHAN!
AWWW! DRUNK CHARLIE! MY FAVOURITE KIND OF CHARLIE!!
NEIL, D'YOU...
KNOCK KNOCK
FINALLY!!

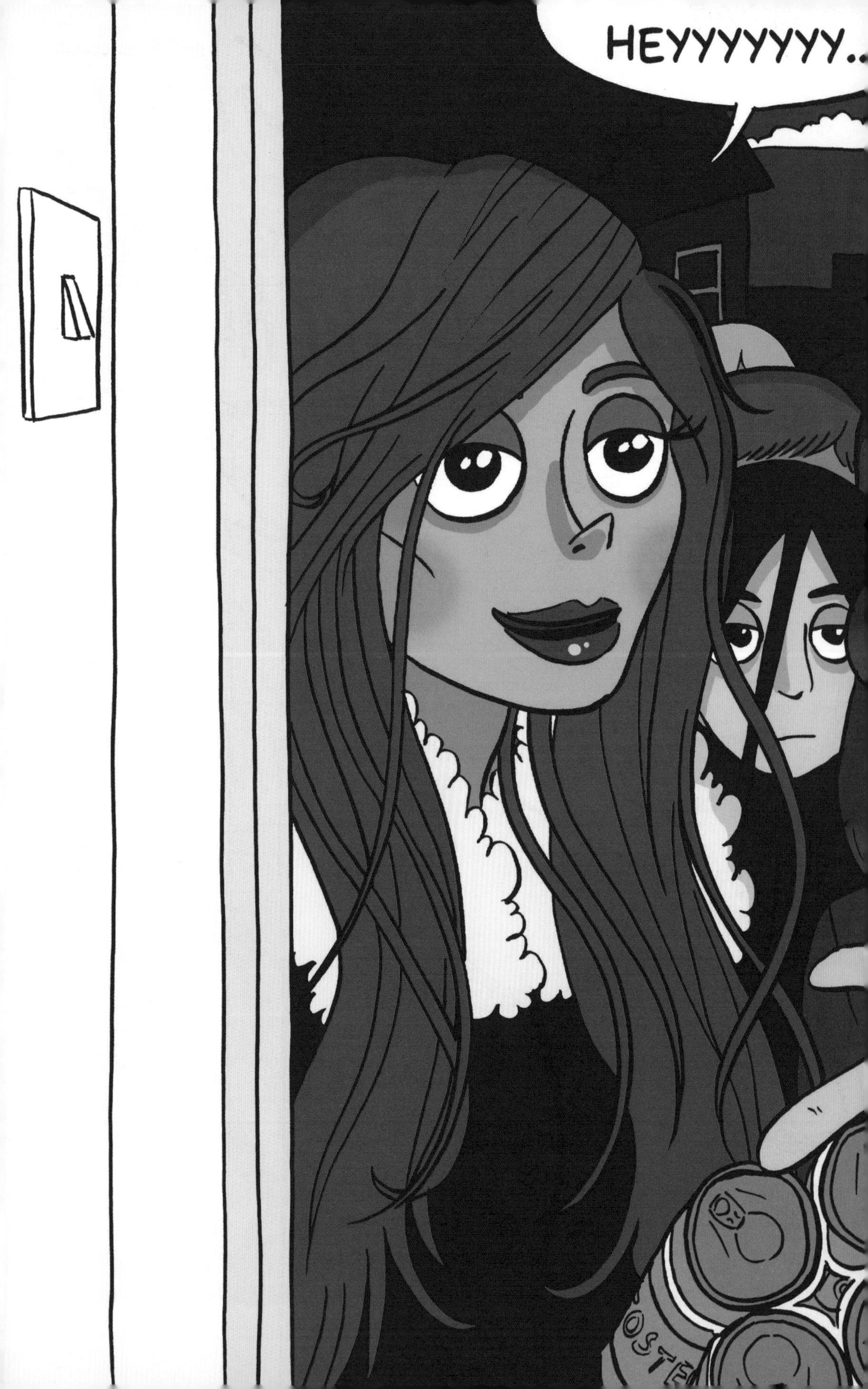
HEYYYYYYY..

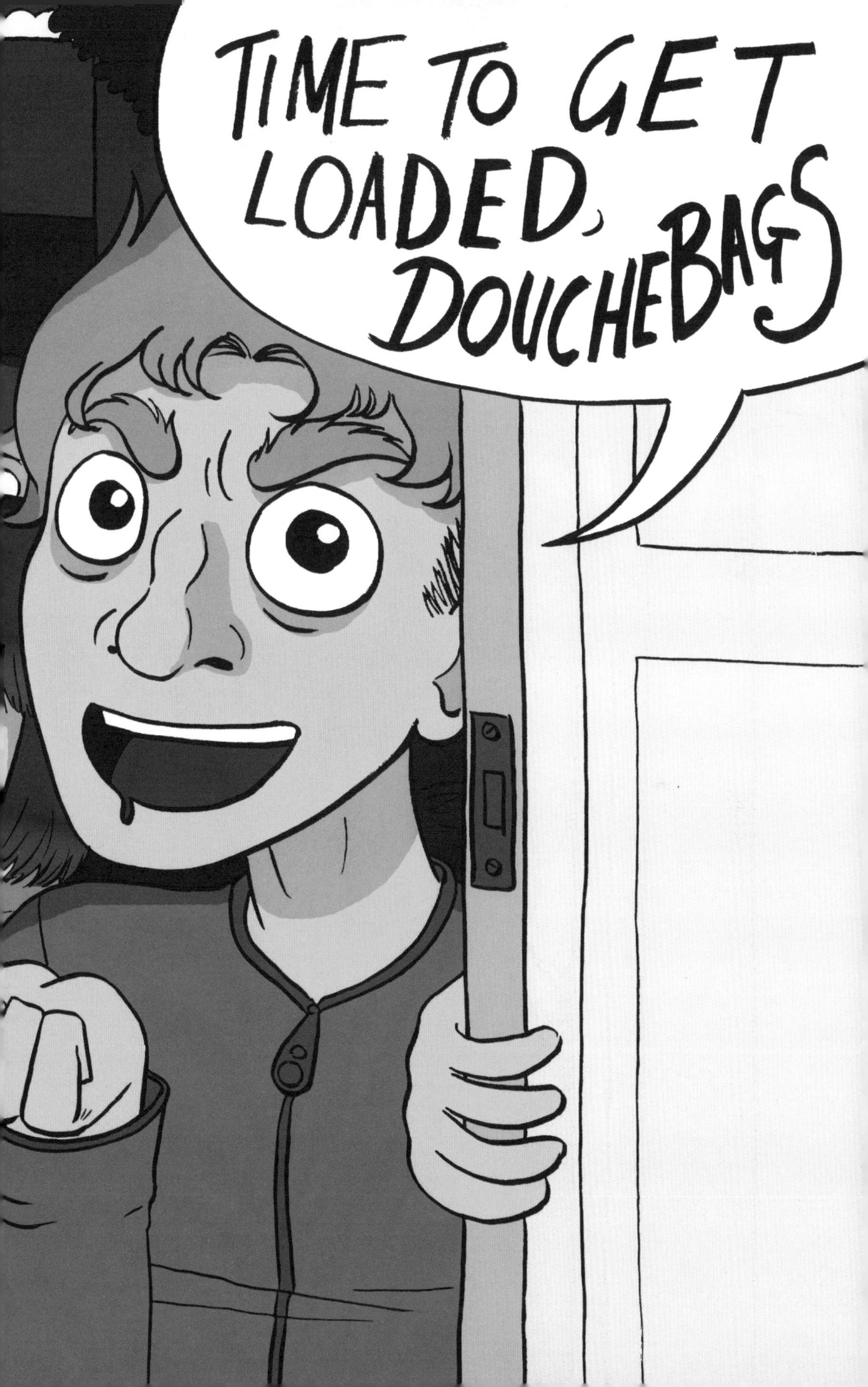
TIME TO GET LOADED, DOUCHEBAGS

CHAPTER TWO

REVELRY

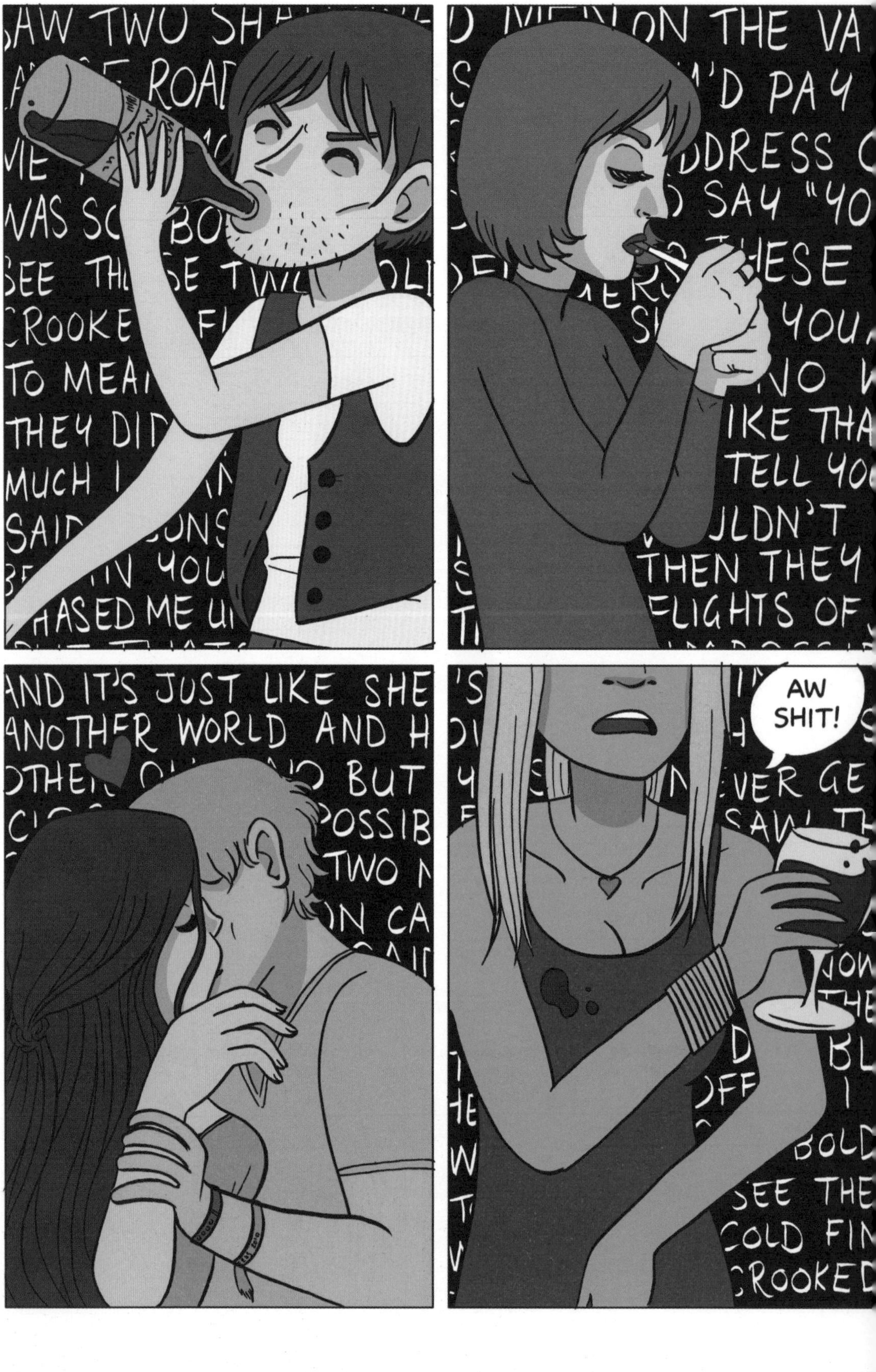
AW SHIT!

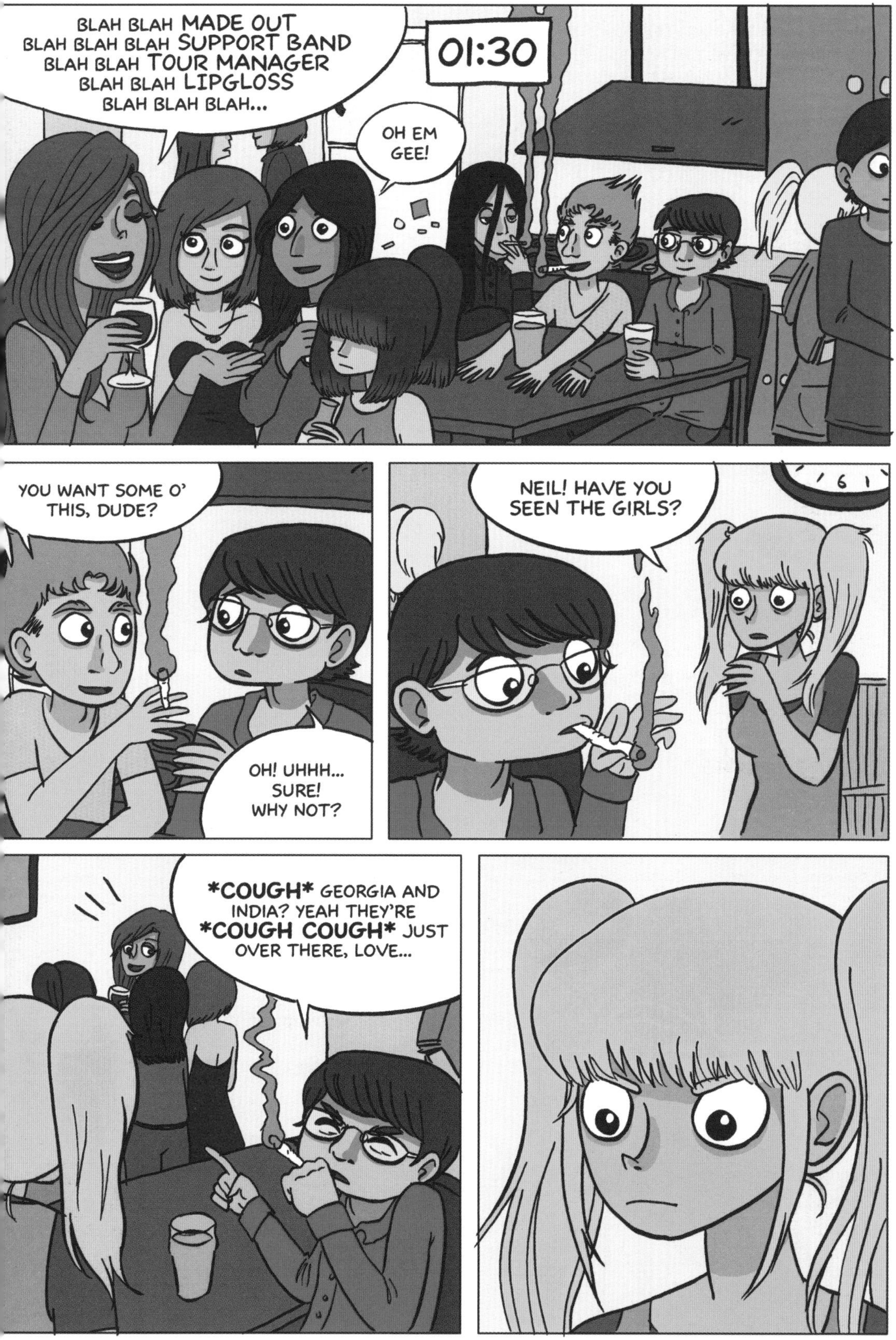
BLAH BLAH MADE OUT BLAH BLAH BLAH SUPPORT BAND BLAH BLAH TOUR MANAGER BLAH BLAH LIPGLOSS BLAH BLAH BLAH...
01:30
OH EM GEE!
YOU WANT SOME O' THIS, DUDE?
OH! UHHH... SURE! WHY NOT?
NEIL! HAVE YOU SEEN THE GIRLS?
COUGH GEORGIA AND INDIA? YEAH THEY'RE *COUGH COUGH* JUST OVER THERE, LOVE...

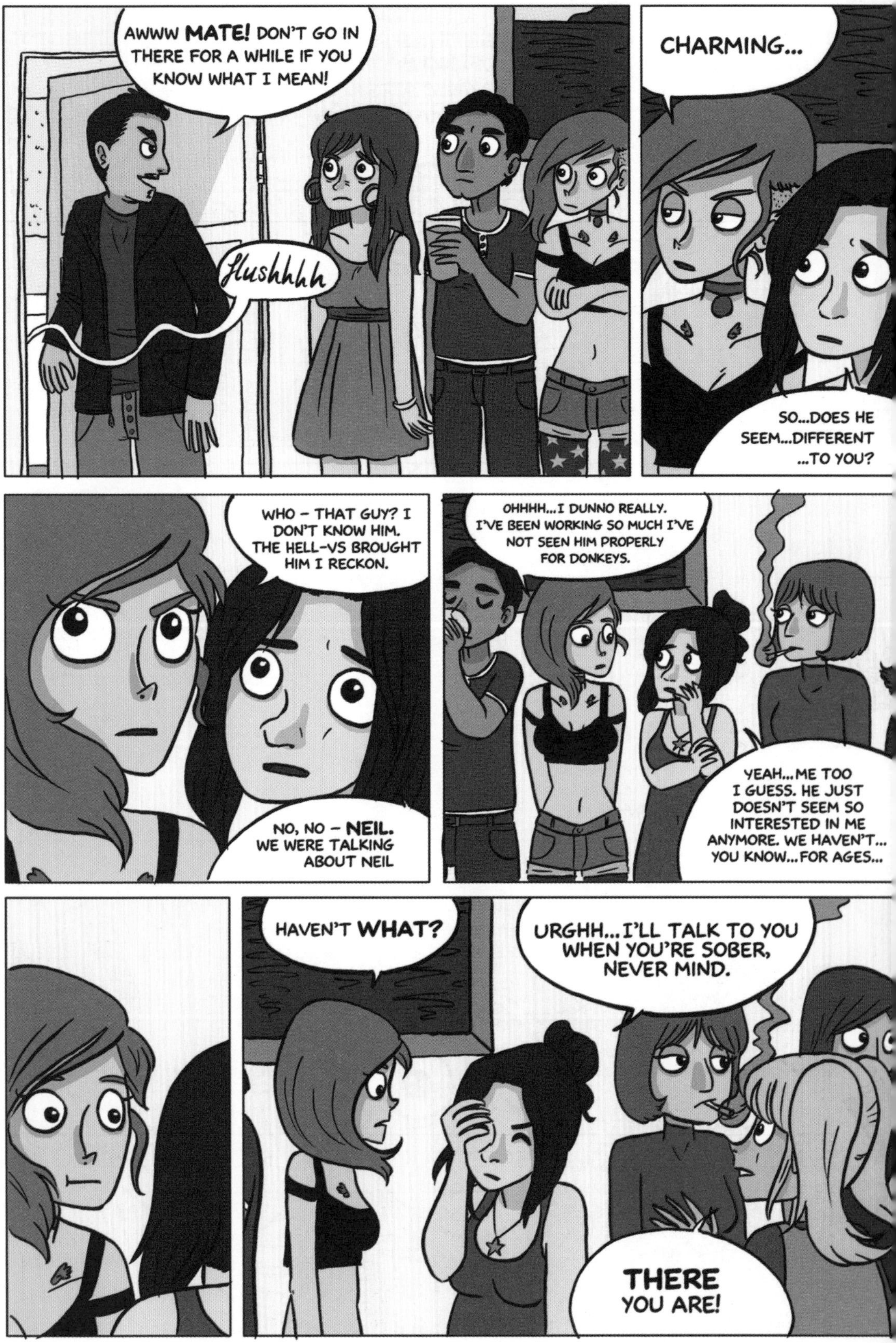
AWWW MATE! DON'T GO IN THERE FOR A WHILE IF YOU KNOW WHAT I MEAN!
Hushhhh
CHARMING...
SO...DOES HE SEEM...DIFFERENT ...TO YOU?
WHO - THAT GUY? I DON'T KNOW HIM. THE HELL-VS BROUGHT HIM I RECKON.
NO, NO - NEIL. WE WERE TALKING ABOUT NEIL
OHHHH...I DUNNO REALLY. I'VE BEEN WORKING SO MUCH I'VE NOT SEEN HIM PROPERLY FOR DONKEYS.
YEAH...ME TOO I GUESS. HE JUST DOESN'T SEEM SO INTERESTED IN ME ANYMORE. WE HAVEN'T... YOU KNOW...FOR AGES...
HAVEN'T WHAT?
URGHH...I'LL TALK TO YOU WHEN YOU'RE SOBER, NEVER MIND.
THERE YOU ARE!

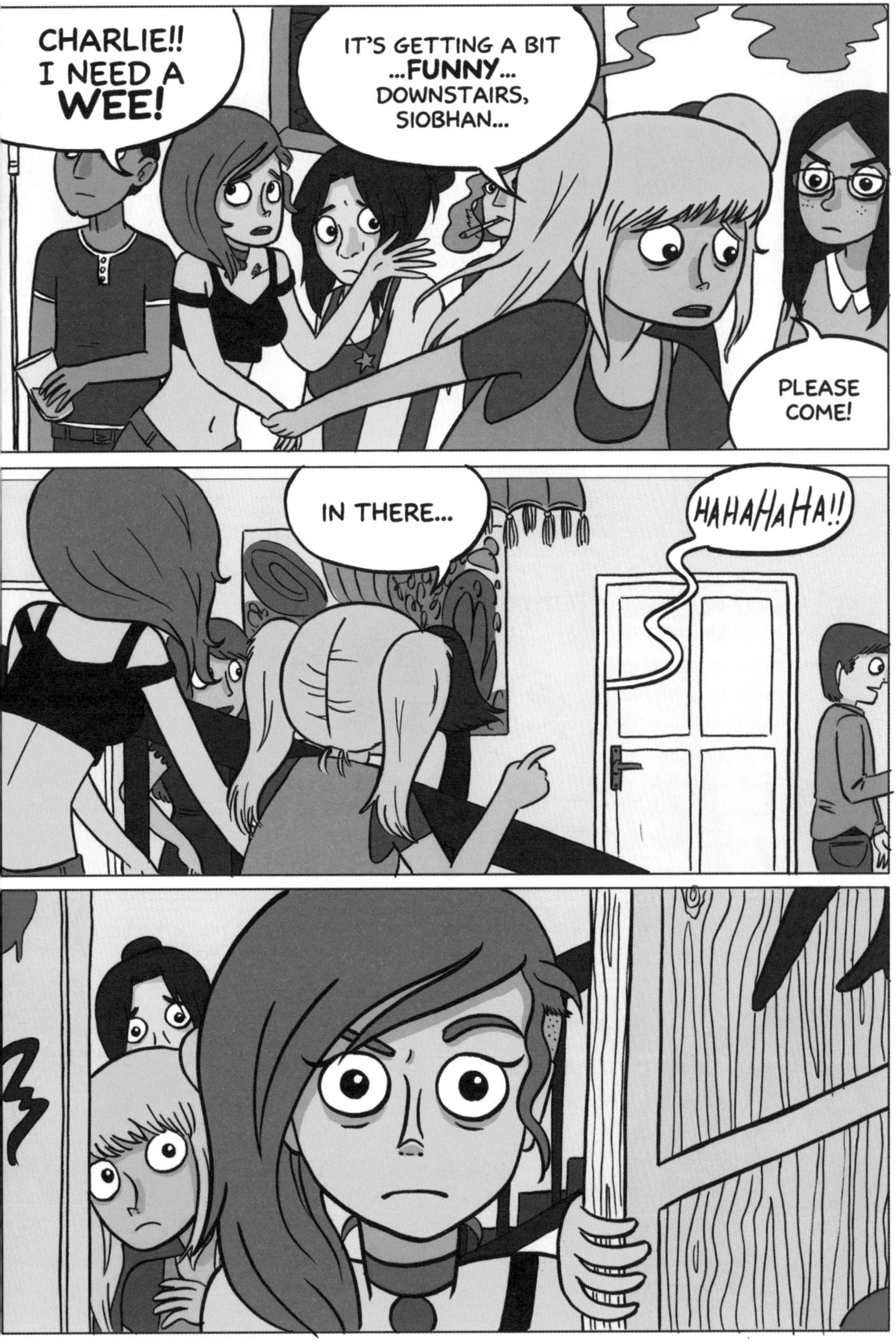
CHARLIE!! I NEED A WEE!
IT'S GETTING A BIT ...FUNNY... DOWNSTAIRS, SIOBHAN...
PLEASE COME!
IN THERE...
HAHAHAHA!!

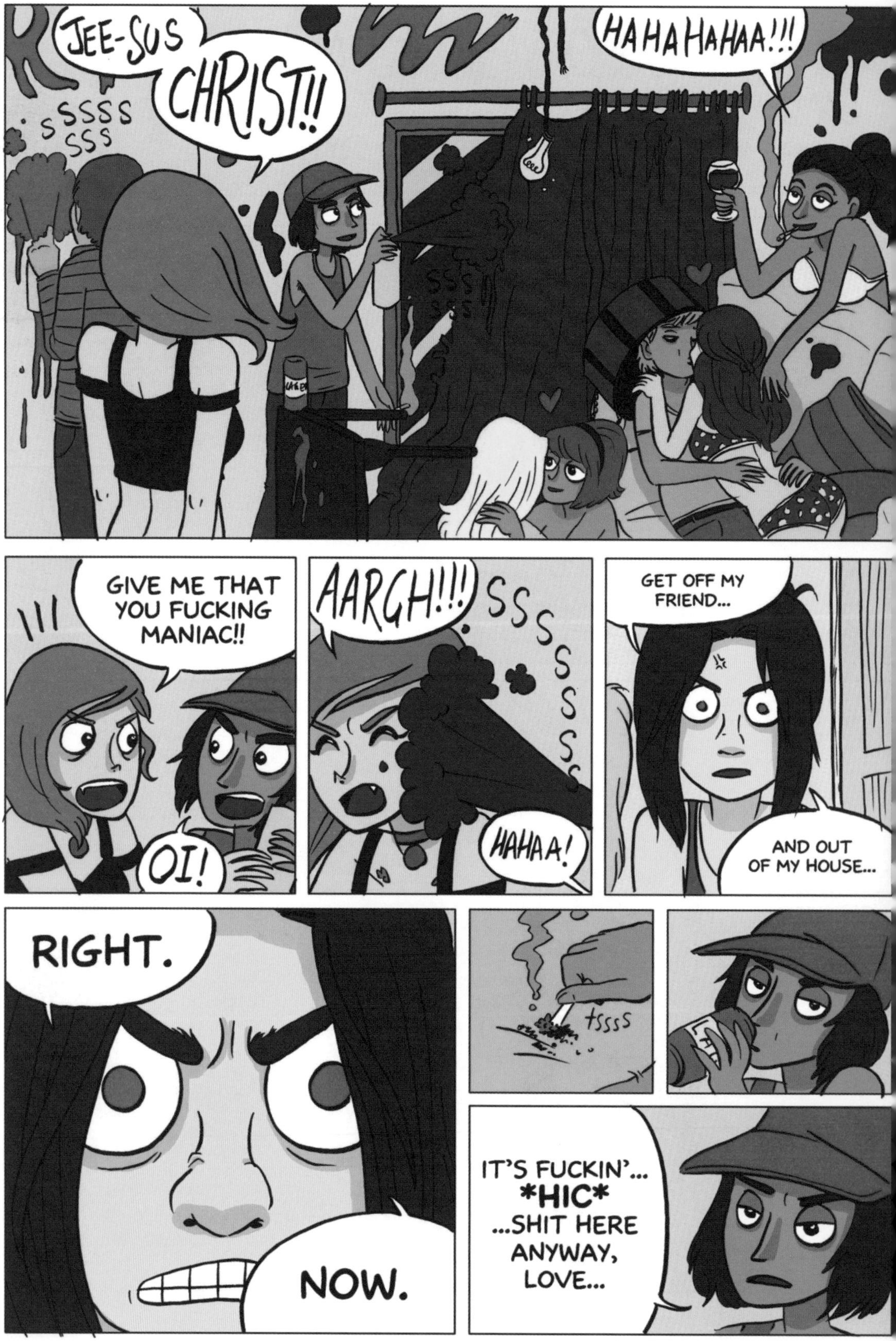
JEE-SUS CHRIST!!
SSSSS SSS
HAHAHAHAA!!!
SSS SSS
GIVE ME THAT YOU FUCKING MANIAC!!
OI!
AARGH!!!
SSSSSSS
HAHAA!
GET OFF MY FRIEND...
AND OUT OF MY HOUSE...
RIGHT.
NOW.
tssss
IT'S FUCKIN'... *HIC* ...SHIT HERE ANYWAY, LOVE...

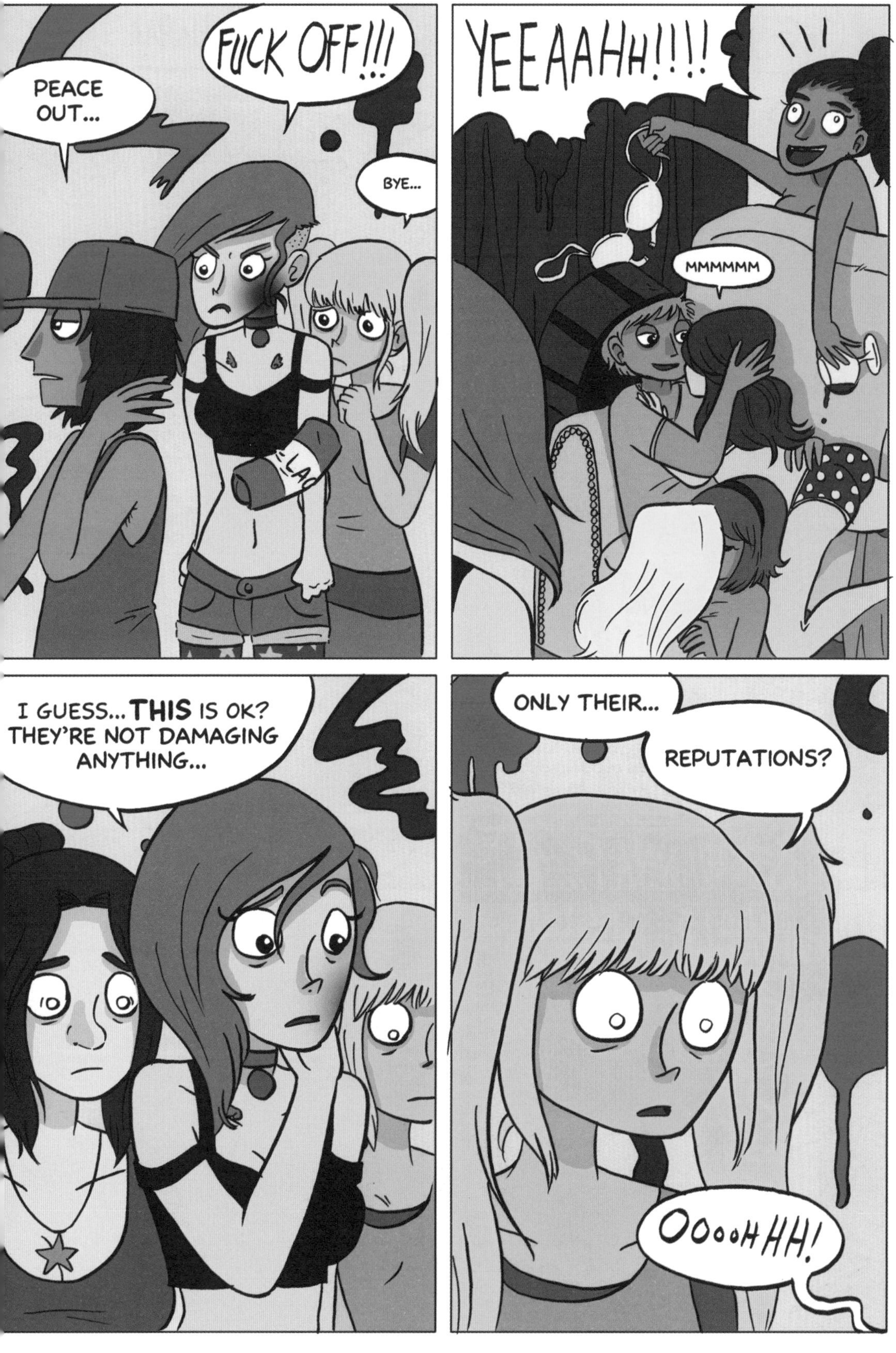
PEACE OUT...
FUCK OFF!!!
BYE...
YEEAAHH!!!!
MMMMMM
I GUESS... **THIS** IS OK? THEY'RE NOT DAMAGING ANYTHING...
ONLY THEIR...
REPUTATIONS?
OOoohHH!

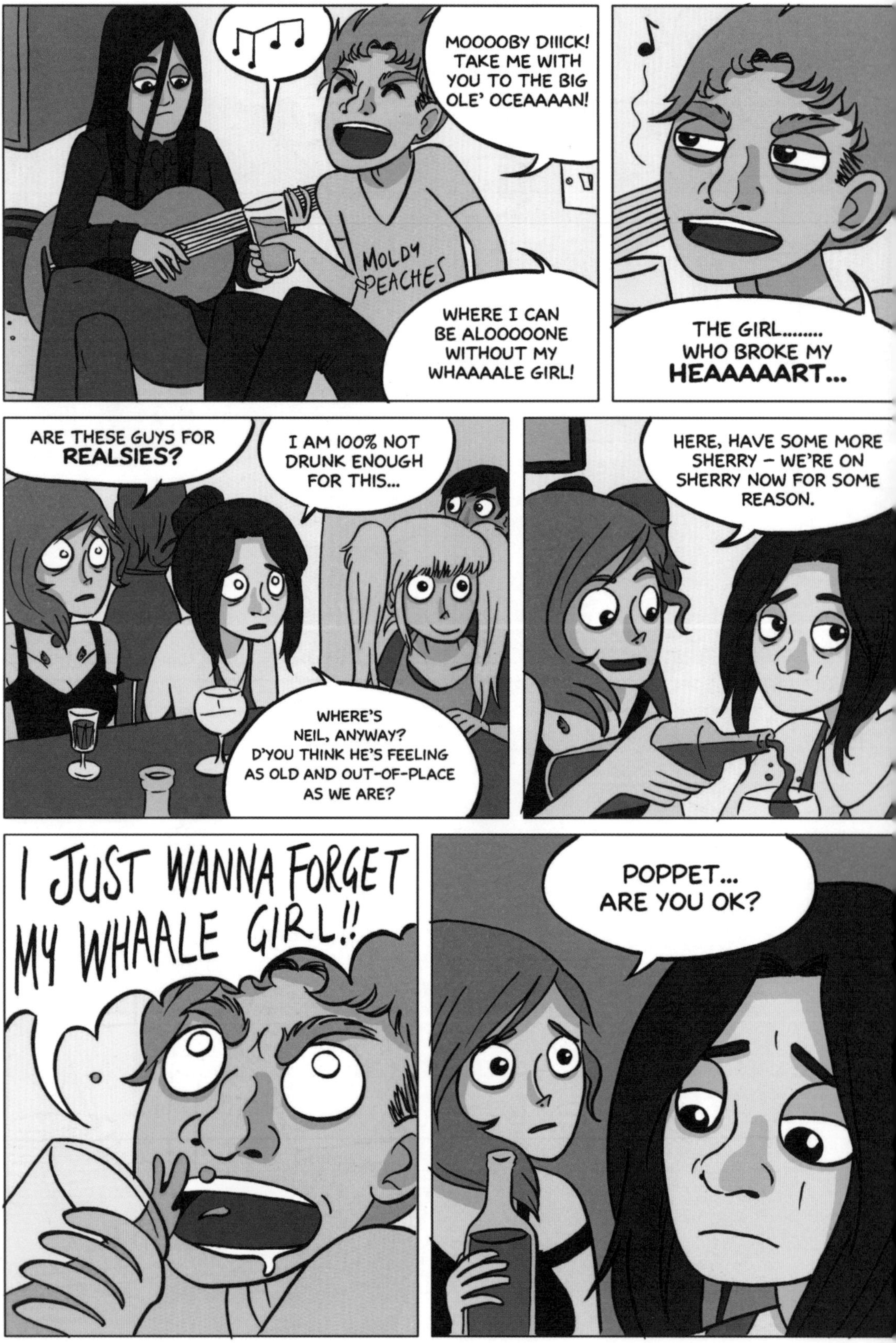
MOOOOBY DIIICK! TAKE ME WITH YOU TO THE BIG OLE' OCEAAAAN!
MOLDY PEACHES
WHERE I CAN BE ALOOOOONE WITHOUT MY WHAAAALE GIRL!
THE GIRL........ WHO BROKE MY HEAAAAART...
ARE THESE GUYS FOR REALSIES?
I AM 100% NOT DRUNK ENOUGH FOR THIS...
WHERE'S NEIL, ANYWAY? D'YOU THINK HE'S FEELING AS OLD AND OUT-OF-PLACE AS WE ARE?
HERE, HAVE SOME MORE SHERRY – WE'RE ON SHERRY NOW FOR SOME REASON.
I JUST WANNA FORGET MY WHAALE GIRL!!
POPPET... ARE YOU OK?

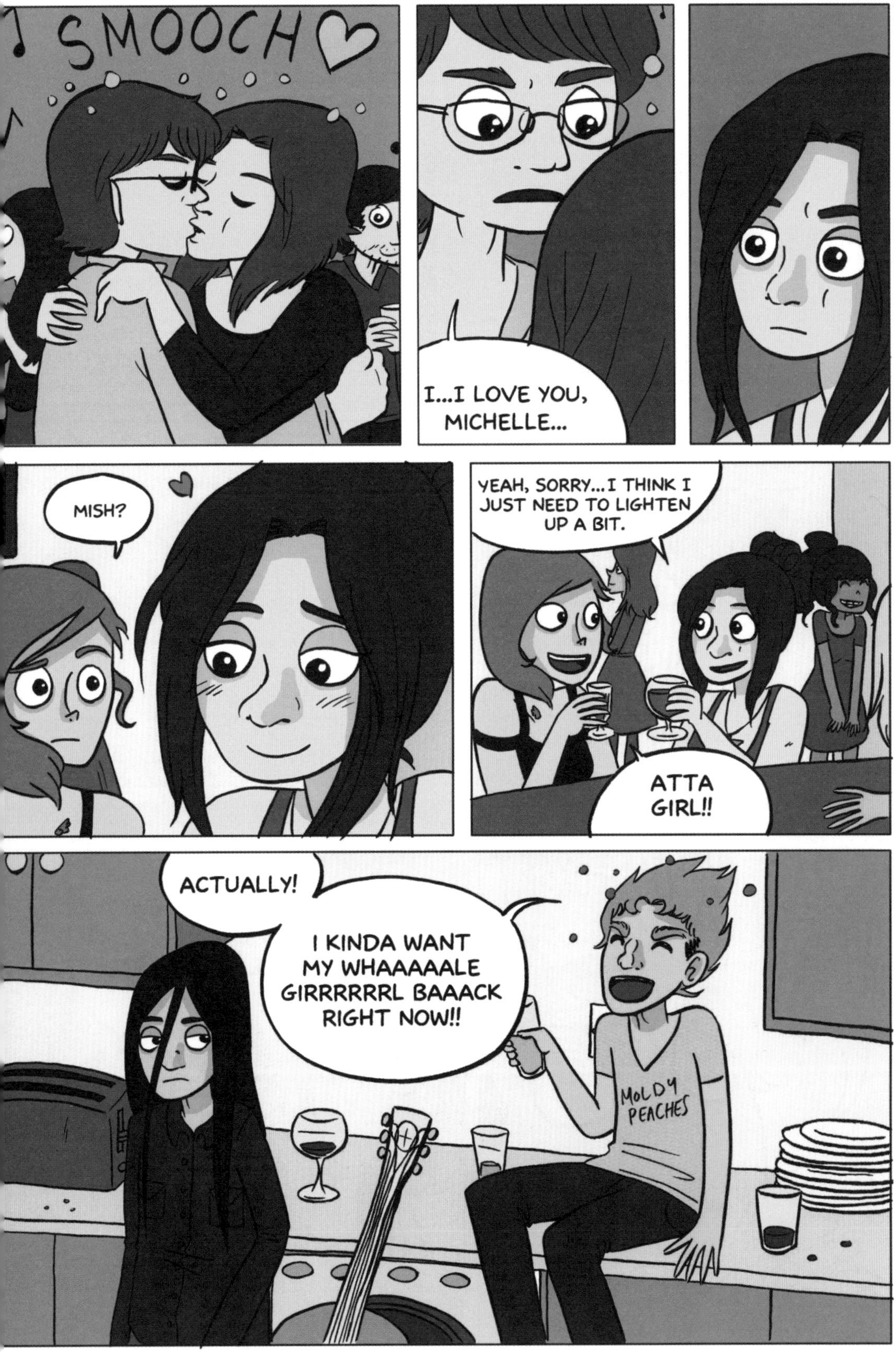
SMOOCH
I...I LOVE YOU, MICHELLE...
MISH?
YEAH, SORRY...I THINK I JUST NEED TO LIGHTEN UP A BIT.
ATTA GIRL!!
ACTUALLY!
I KINDA WANT MY WHAAAAALE GIRRRRRRL BAAACK RIGHT NOW!!
MOLDY PEACHES

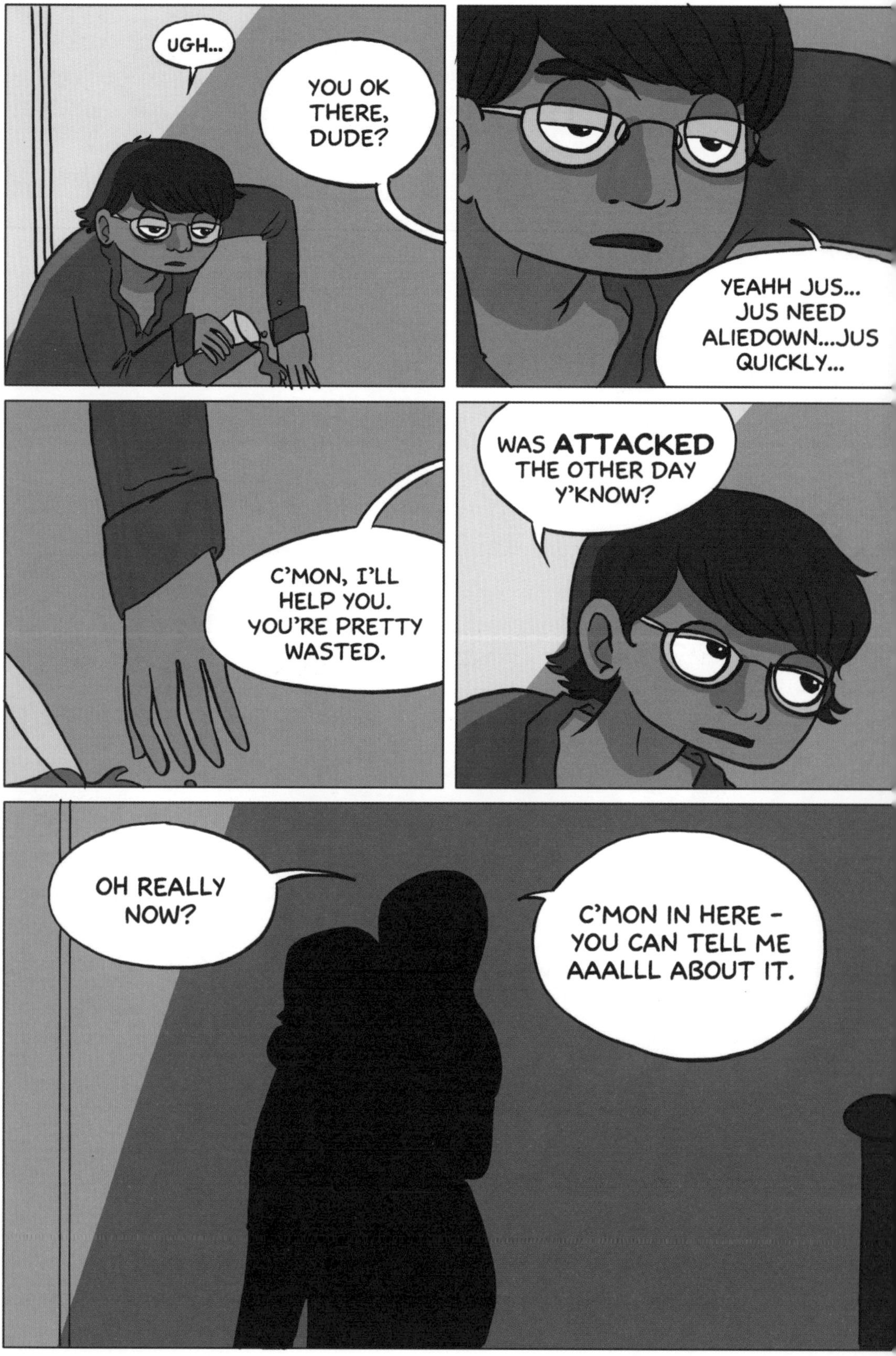
UGH...
YOU OK THERE, DUDE?
YEAHH JUS... JUS NEED ALIEDOWN...JUS QUICKLY...
C'MON, I'LL HELP YOU. YOU'RE PRETTY WASTED.
WAS **ATTACKED** THE OTHER DAY Y'KNOW?
OH REALLY NOW?
C'MON IN HERE - YOU CAN TELL ME AAALLL ABOUT IT.

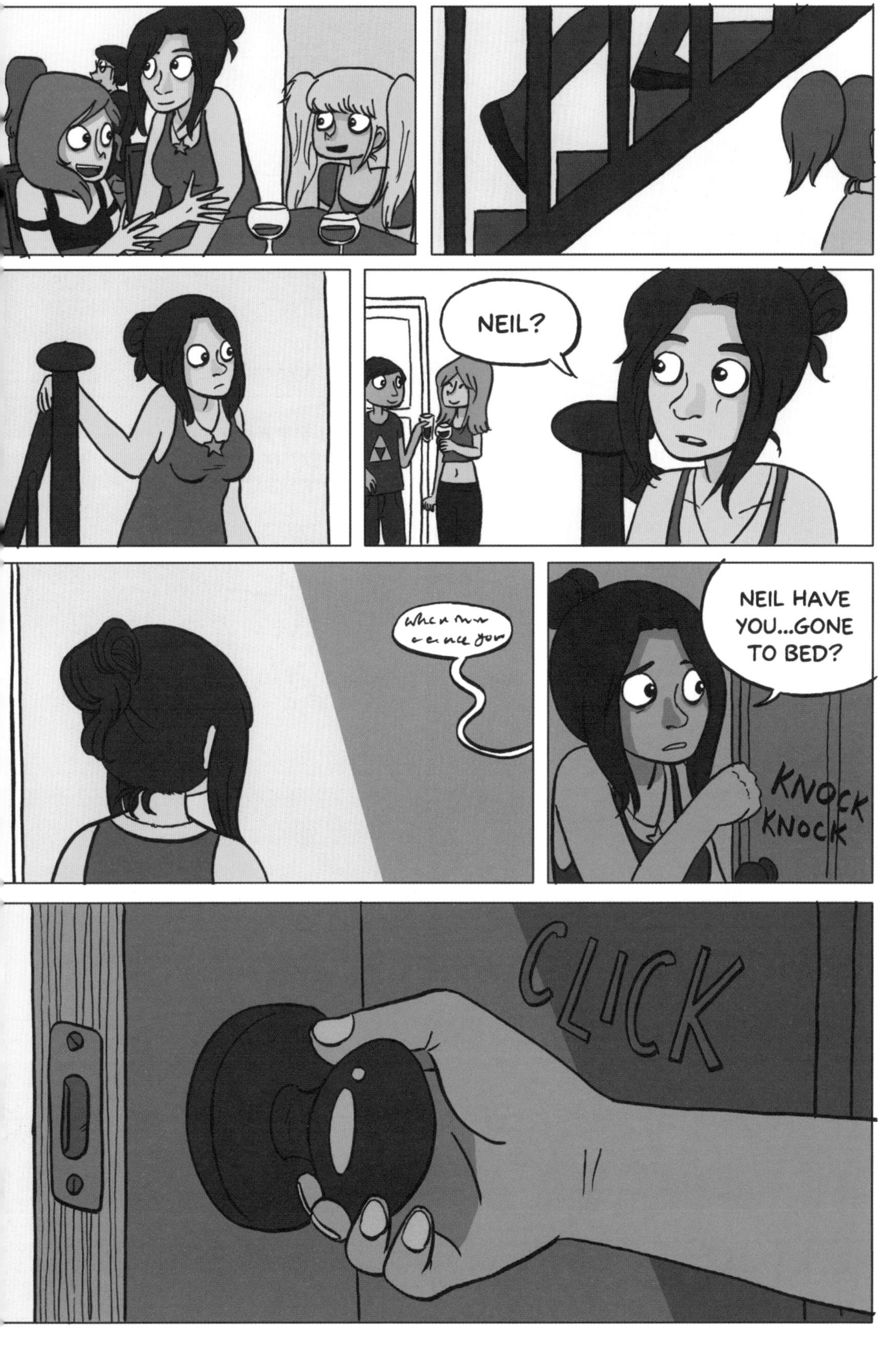
NEIL?
NEIL HAVE YOU...GONE TO BED?
KNOCK KNOCK
CLICK

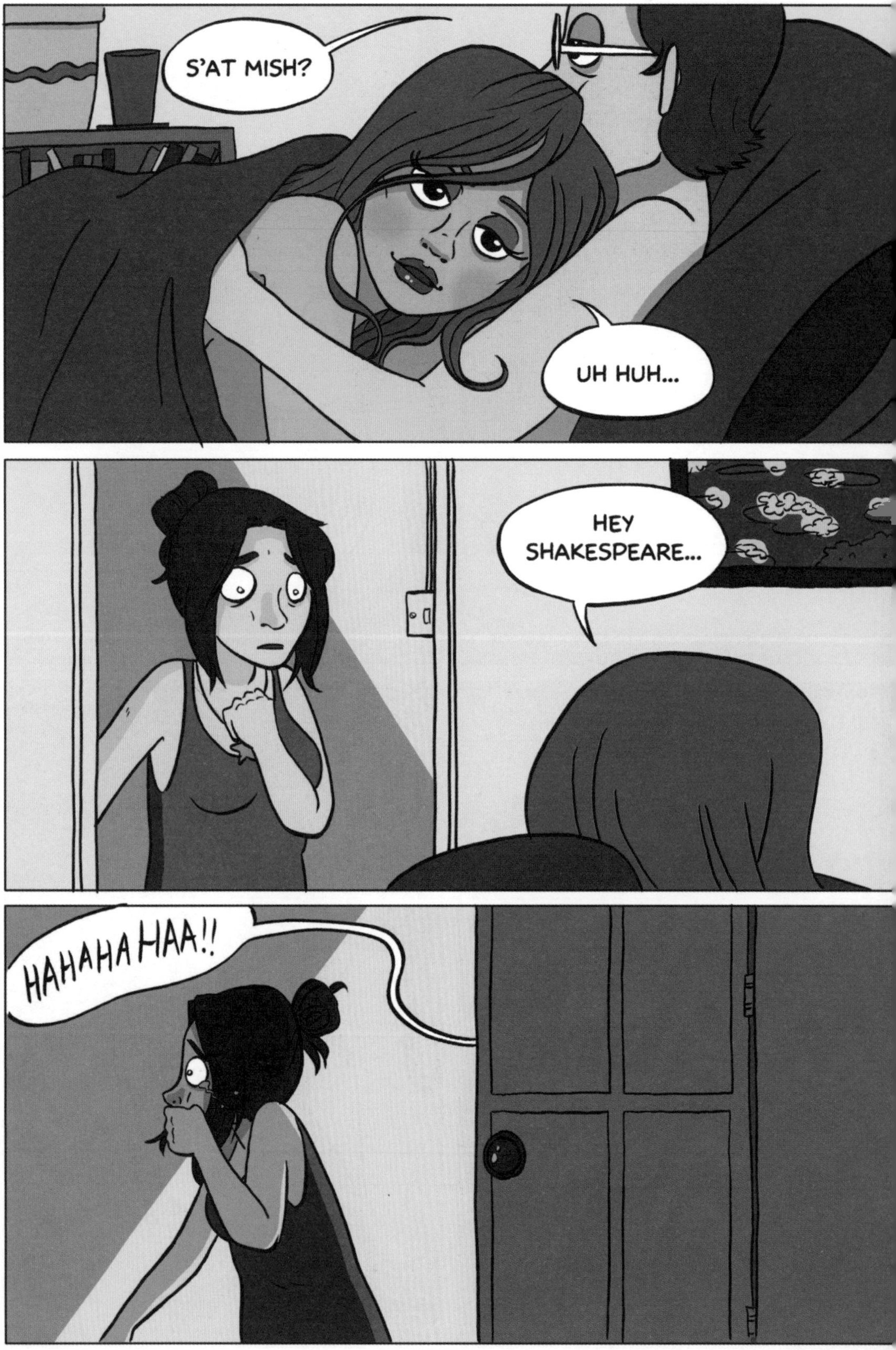
S'AT MISH?
UH HUH...
HEY SHAKESPEARE...
HAHAHA HAA!!

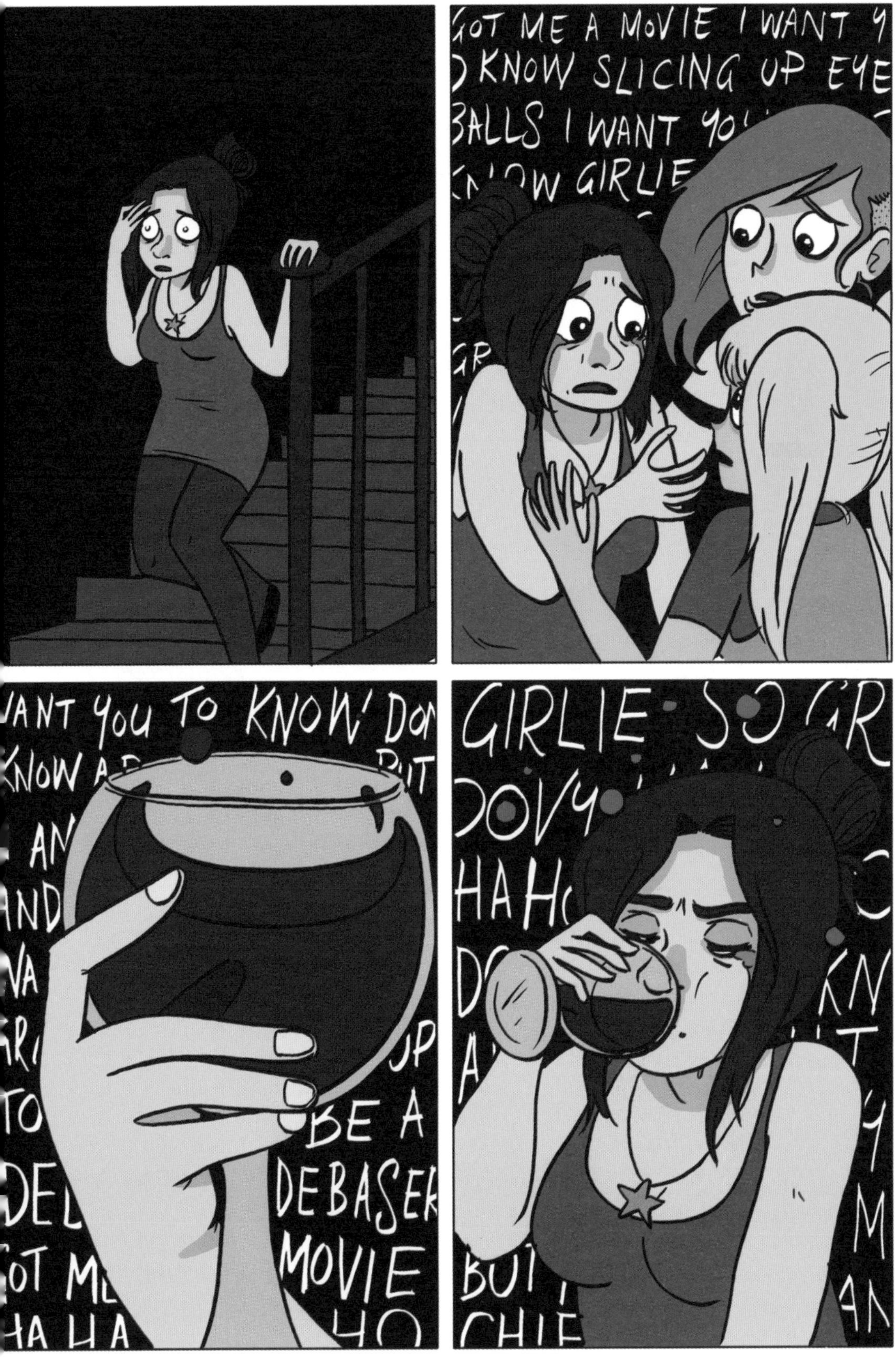
ME A MOVIE I WANT
KNOW SLICING UP EYE
BALLS I WANT
GIRLIE
WANT YOU TO KNOW
BE A
DEBASER
MOVIE
HA HA
GIRLIE
DOVY
HA H
BUT

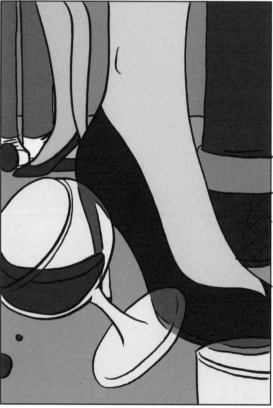

MISH...?

CHAPTER THREE

AFTERMATH

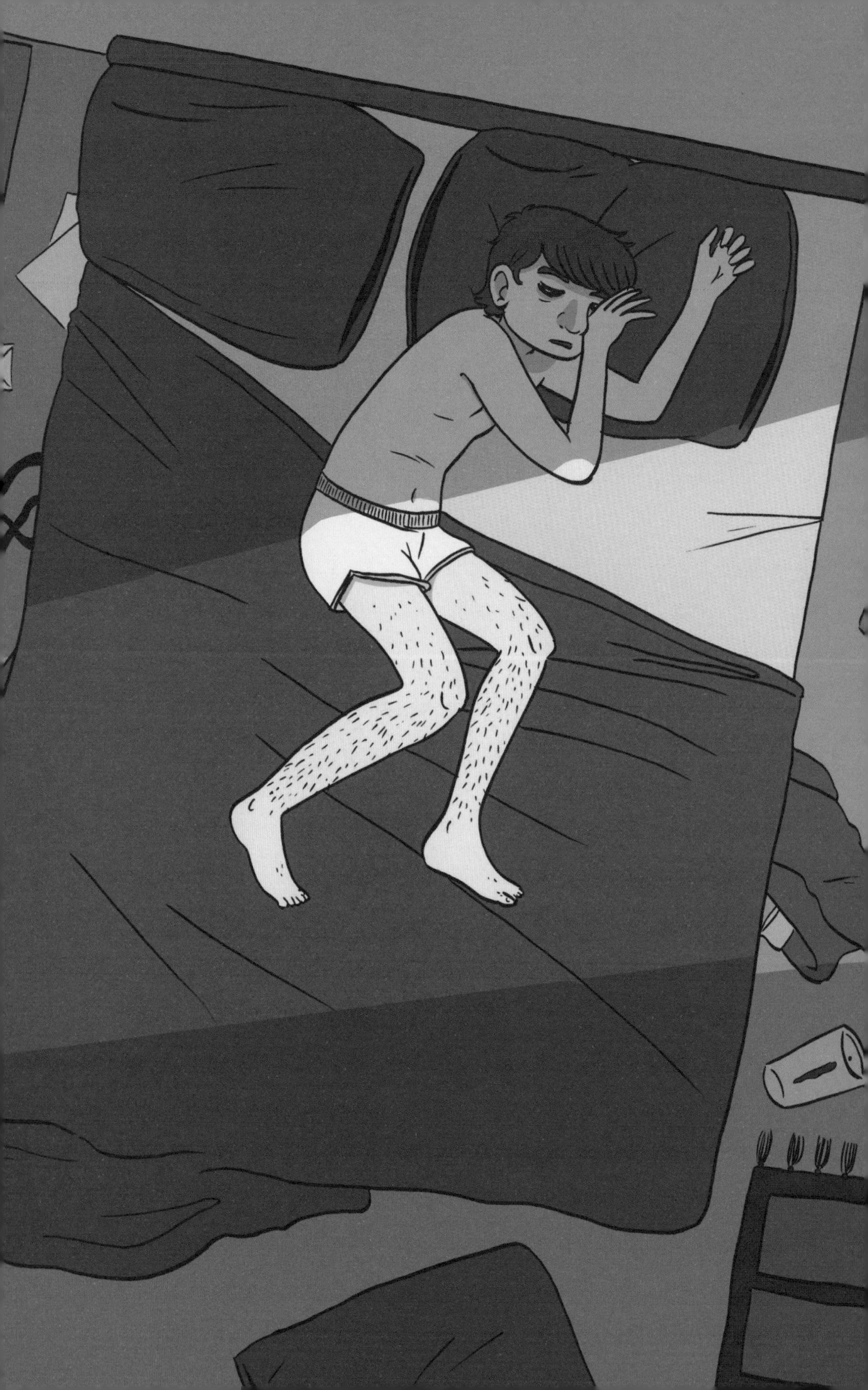

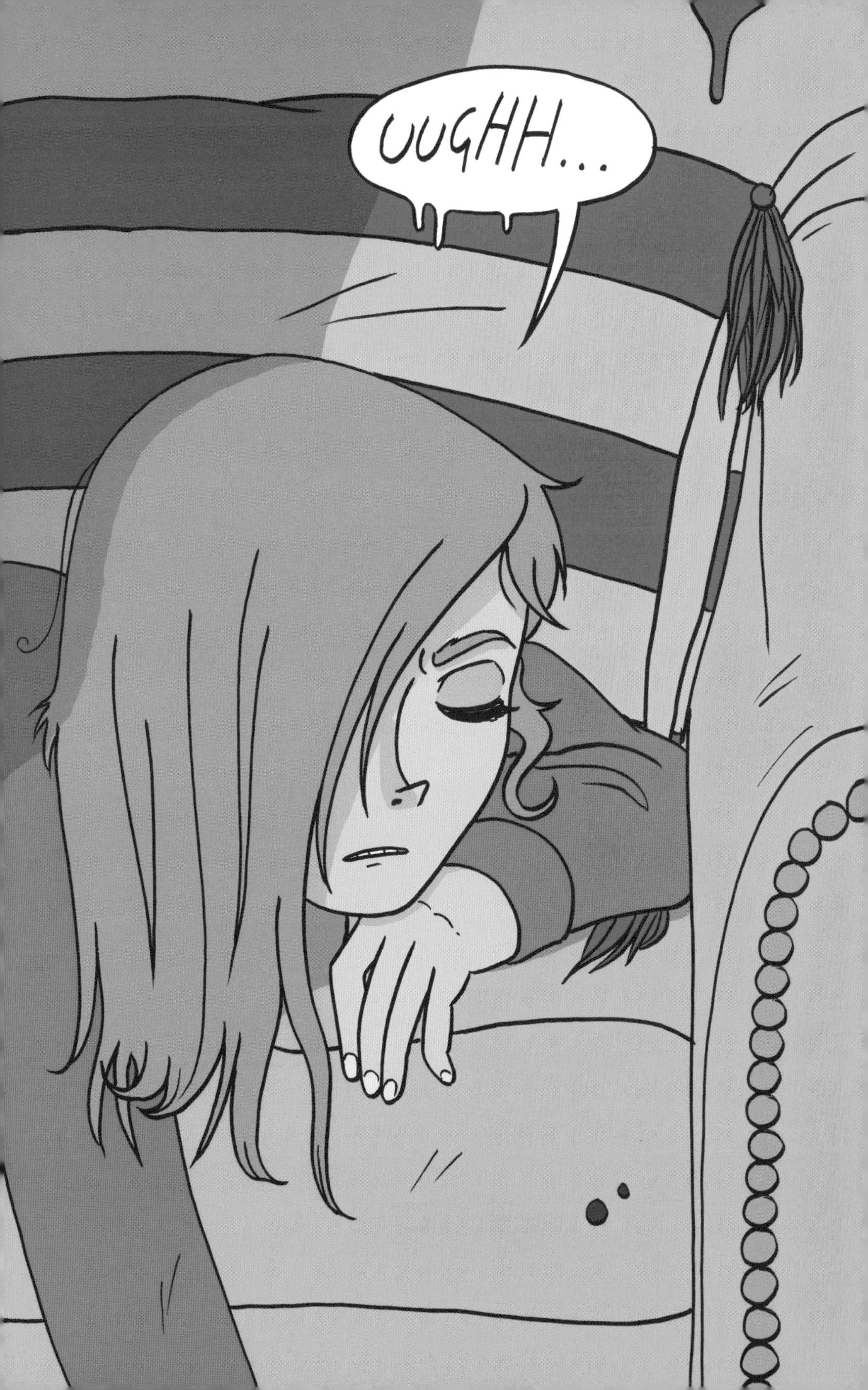
UUGHH...

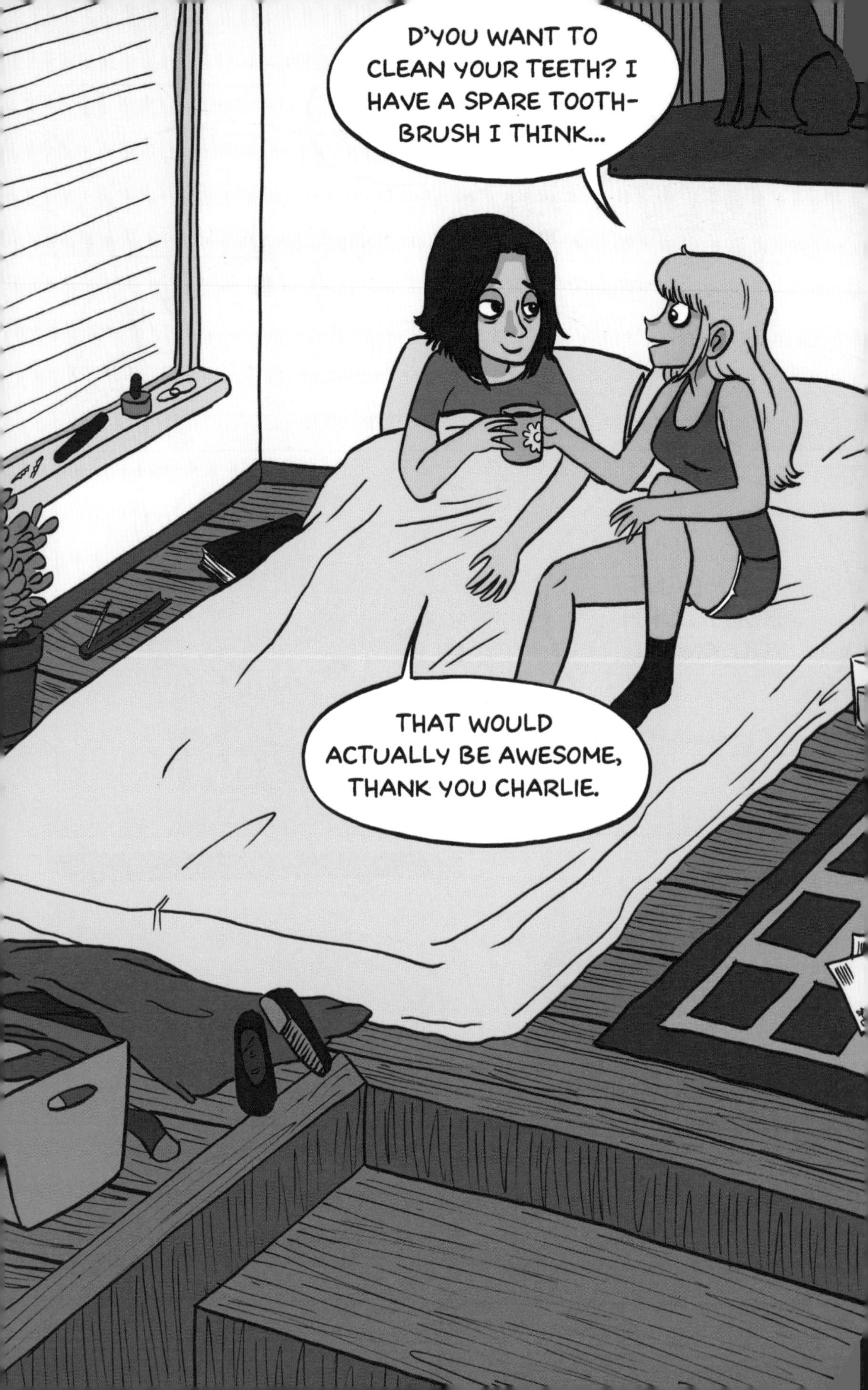
D'YOU WANT TO CLEAN YOUR TEETH? I HAVE A SPARE TOOTH-BRUSH I THINK...
THAT WOULD ACTUALLY BE AWESOME, THANK YOU CHARLIE.

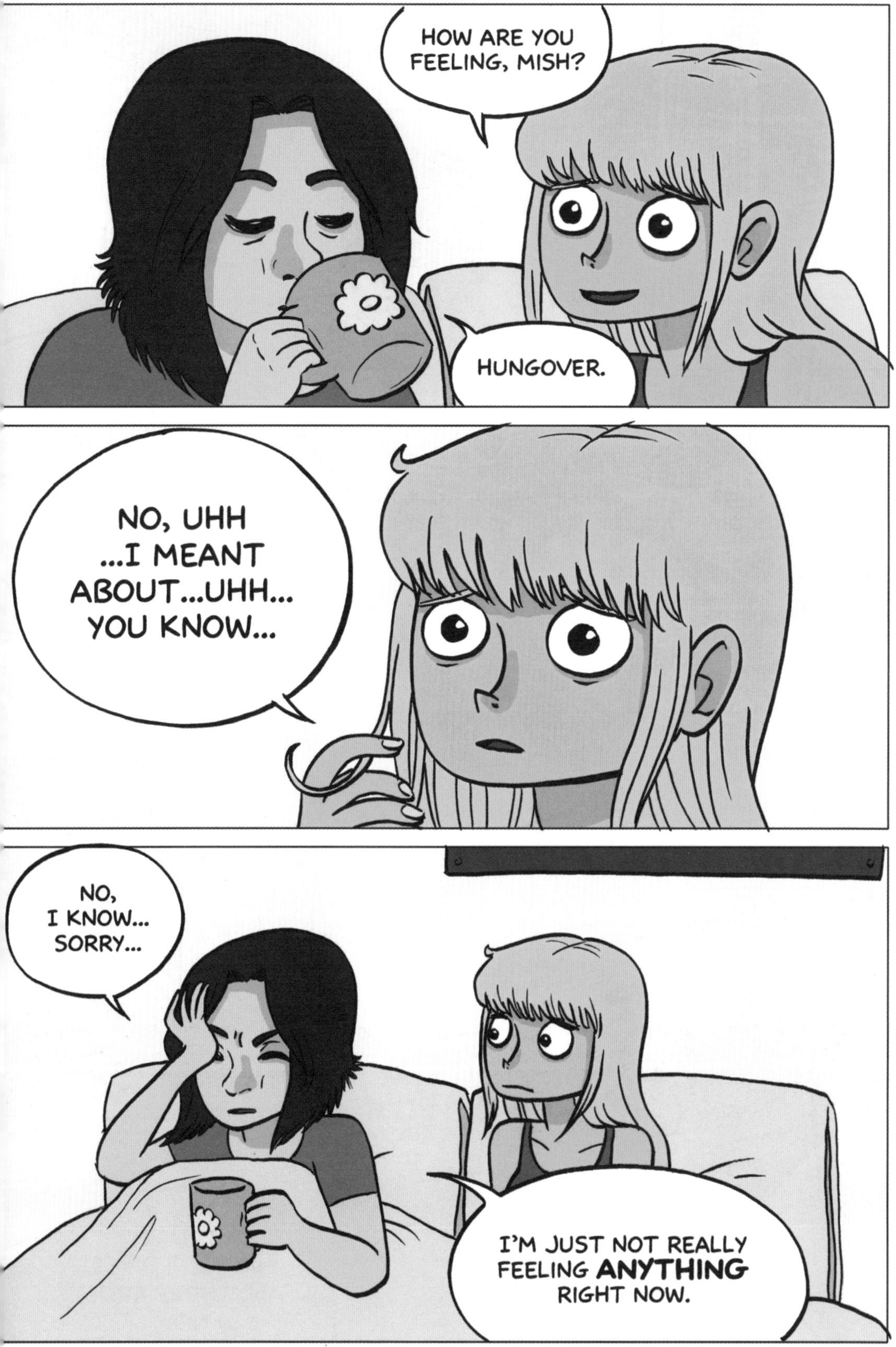
HOW ARE YOU FEELING, MISH?
HUNGOVER.
NO, UHH ...I MEANT ABOUT...UHH... YOU KNOW...
NO, I KNOW... SORRY...
I'M JUST NOT REALLY FEELING **ANYTHING** RIGHT NOW.

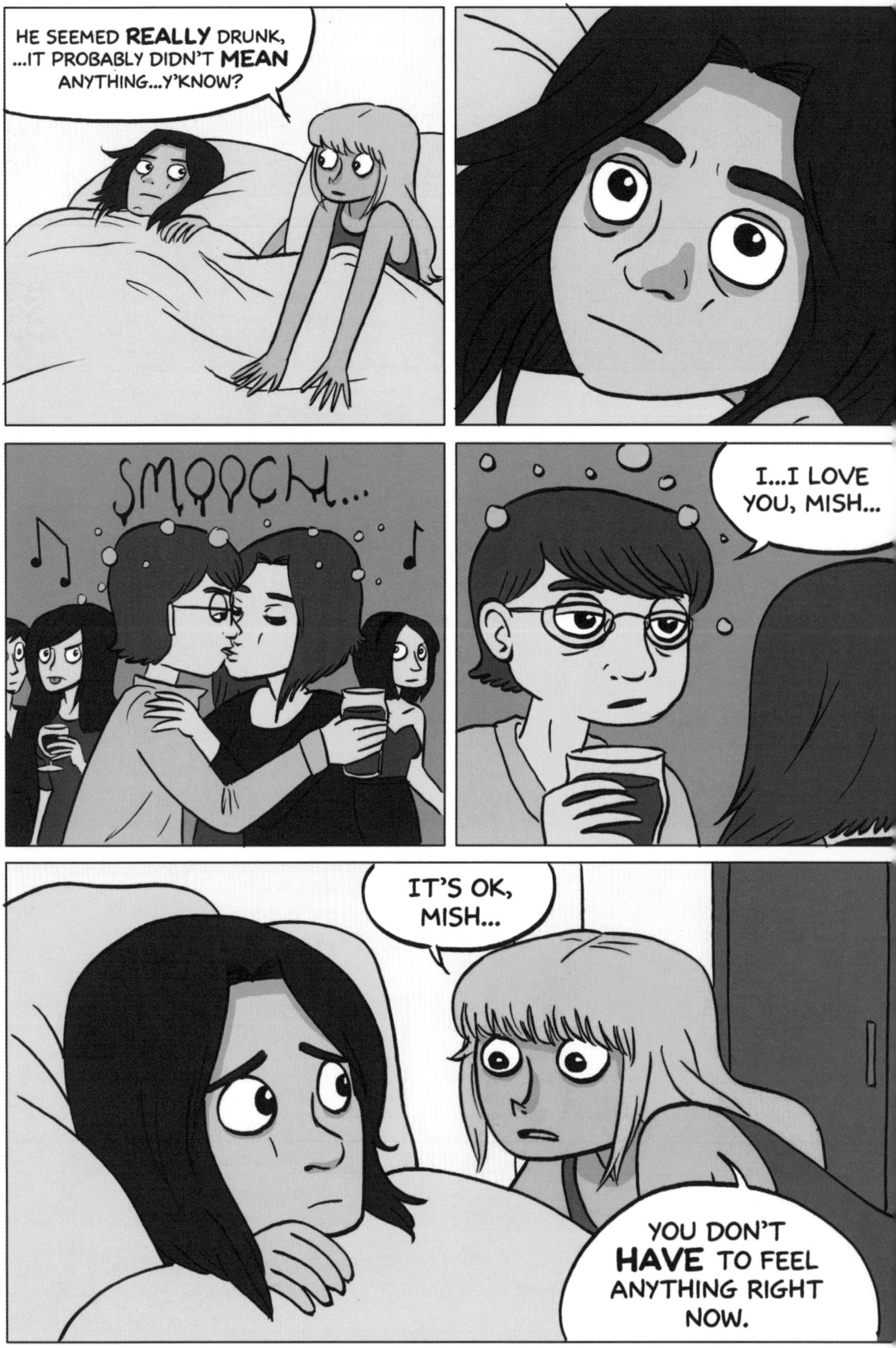
HE SEEMED **REALLY** DRUNK, ...IT PROBABLY DIDN'T **MEAN** ANYTHING...Y'KNOW?
SMOOCH...
I...I LOVE YOU, MISH...
IT'S OK, MISH...
YOU DON'T **HAVE** TO FEEL ANYTHING RIGHT NOW.

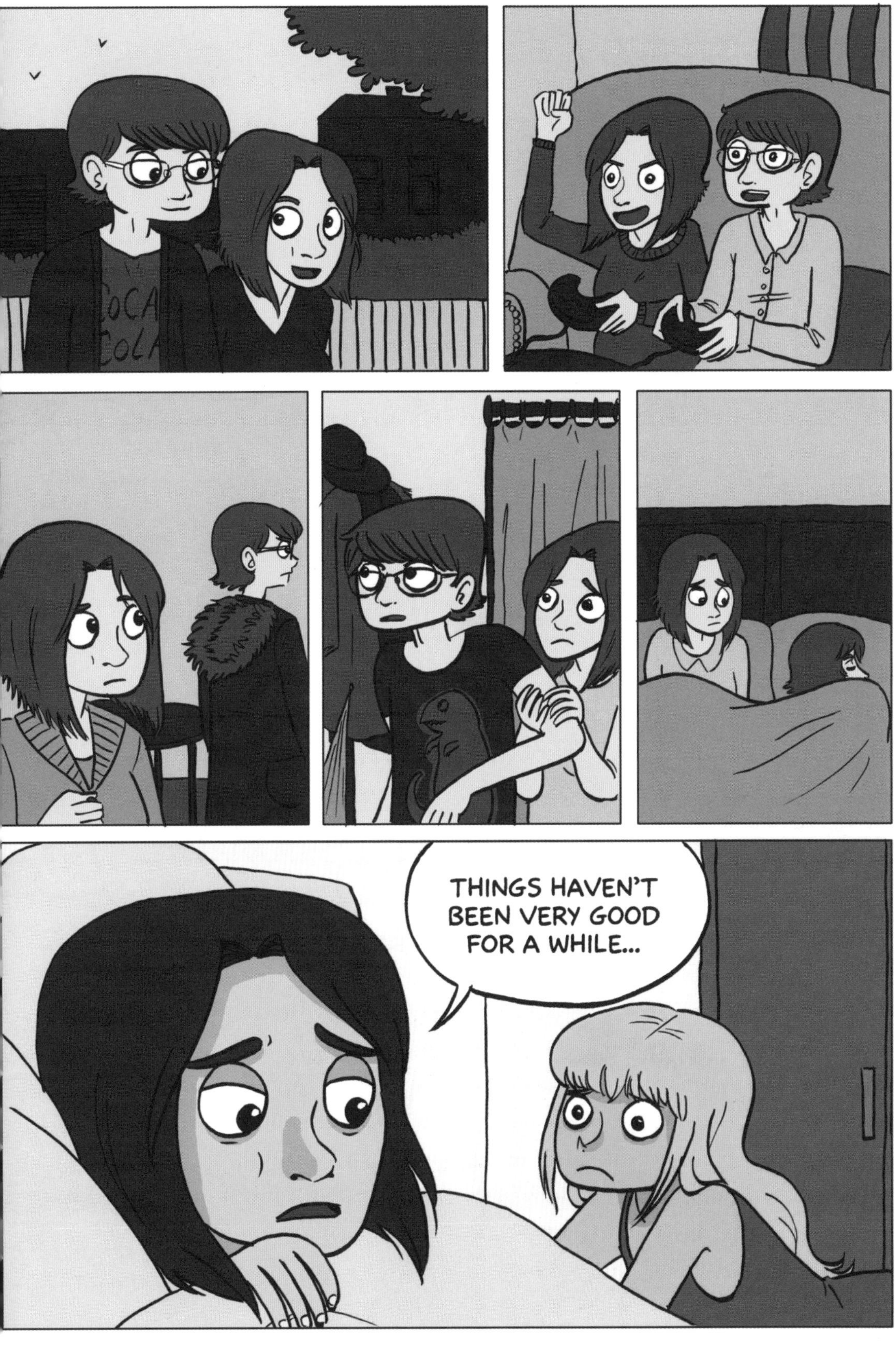

COCA COLA
THINGS HAVEN'T BEEN VERY GOOD FOR A WHILE...

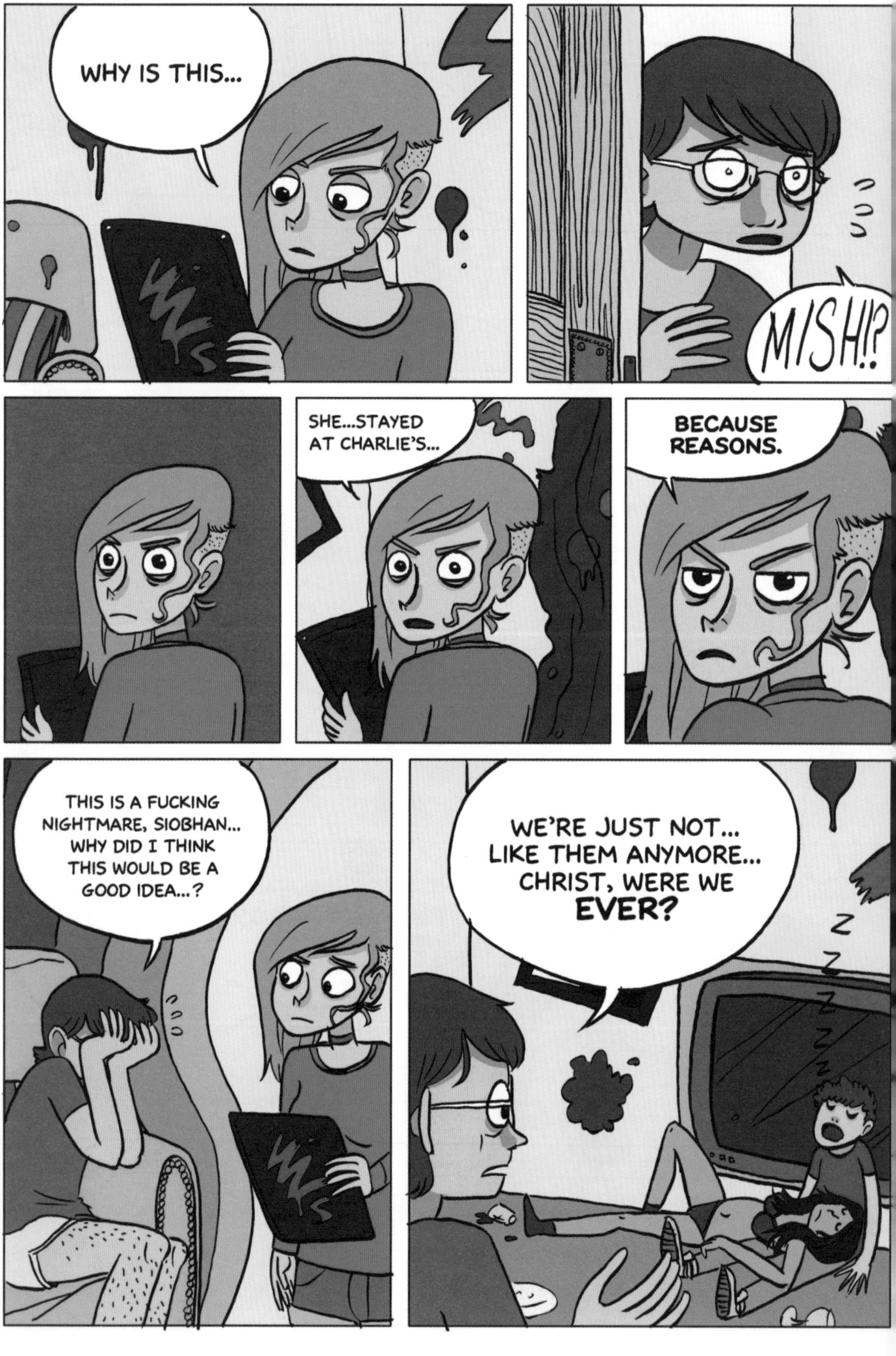
WHY IS THIS...
MISH!?
SHE...STAYED AT CHARLIE'S...
BECAUSE REASONS.
THIS IS A FUCKING NIGHTMARE, SIOBHAN... WHY DID I THINK THIS WOULD BE A GOOD IDEA...?
WE'RE JUST NOT... LIKE THEM ANYMORE... CHRIST, WERE WE EVER?
Z Z Z Z Z Z

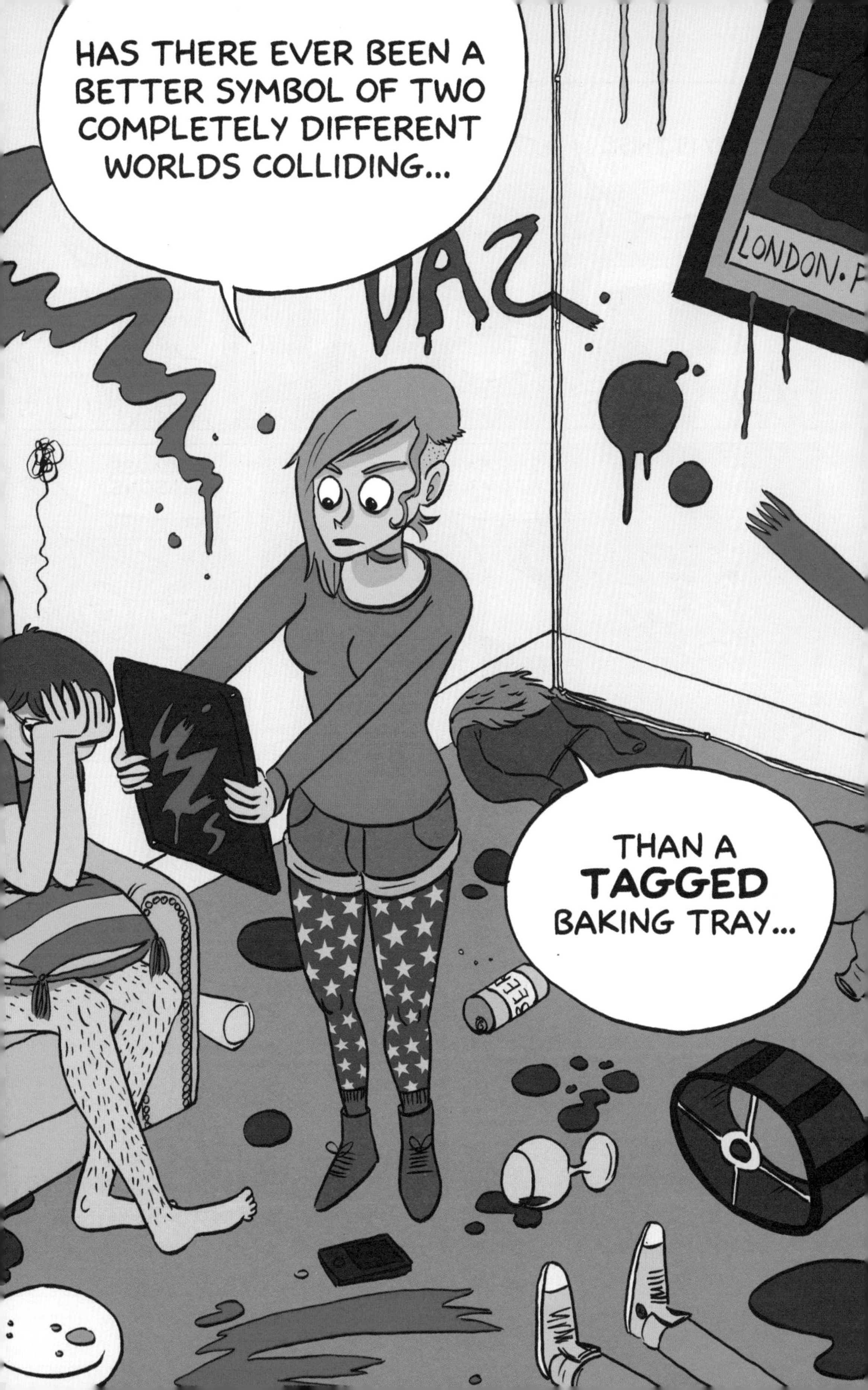
HAS THERE EVER BEEN A BETTER SYMBOL OF TWO COMPLETELY DIFFERENT WORLDS COLLIDING...
DAZ
LONDON•P
THAN A **TAGGED** BAKING TRAY...
BEER

EPILOGUE

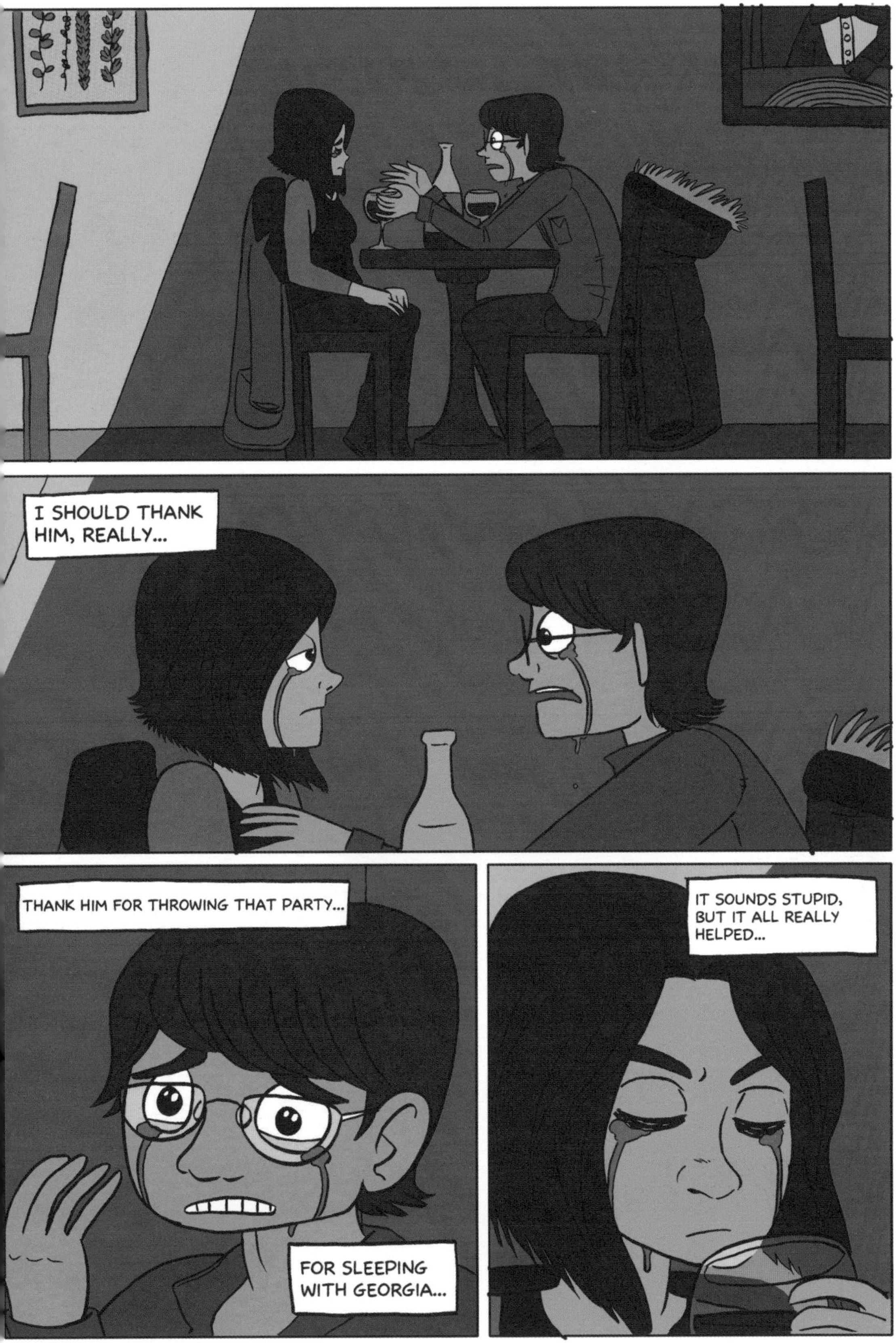
I SHOULD THANK HIM, REALLY...
THANK HIM FOR THROWING THAT PARTY...
FOR SLEEPING WITH GEORGIA...
IT SOUNDS STUPID, BUT IT ALL REALLY HELPED...

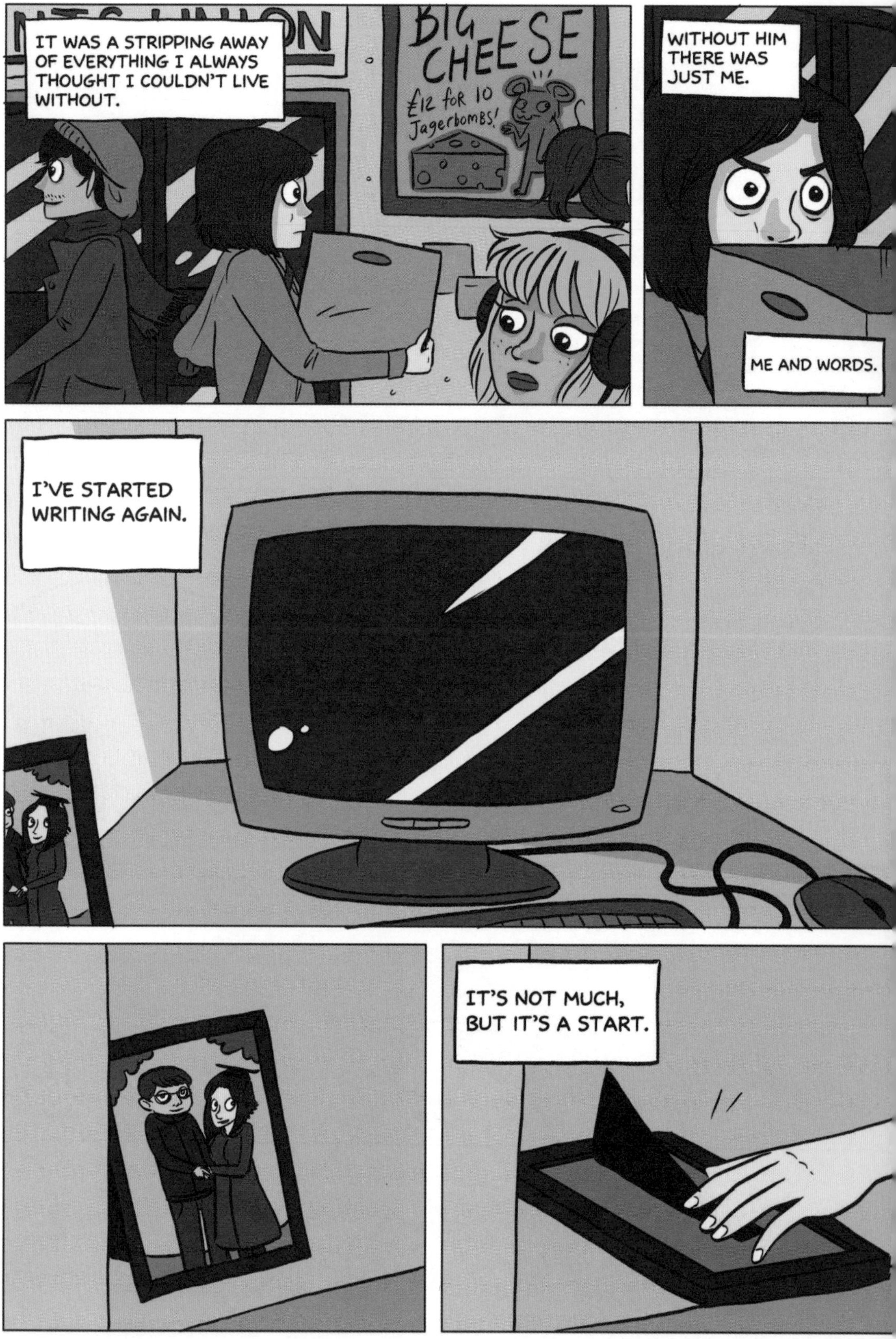

IT WAS A STRIPPING AWAY OF EVERYTHING I ALWAYS THOUGHT I COULDN'T LIVE WITHOUT.
BIG CHEESE
£12 for 10 Jagerbombs!
WITHOUT HIM THERE WAS JUST ME.
ME AND WORDS.
I'VE STARTED WRITING AGAIN.
IT'S NOT MUCH, BUT IT'S A START.

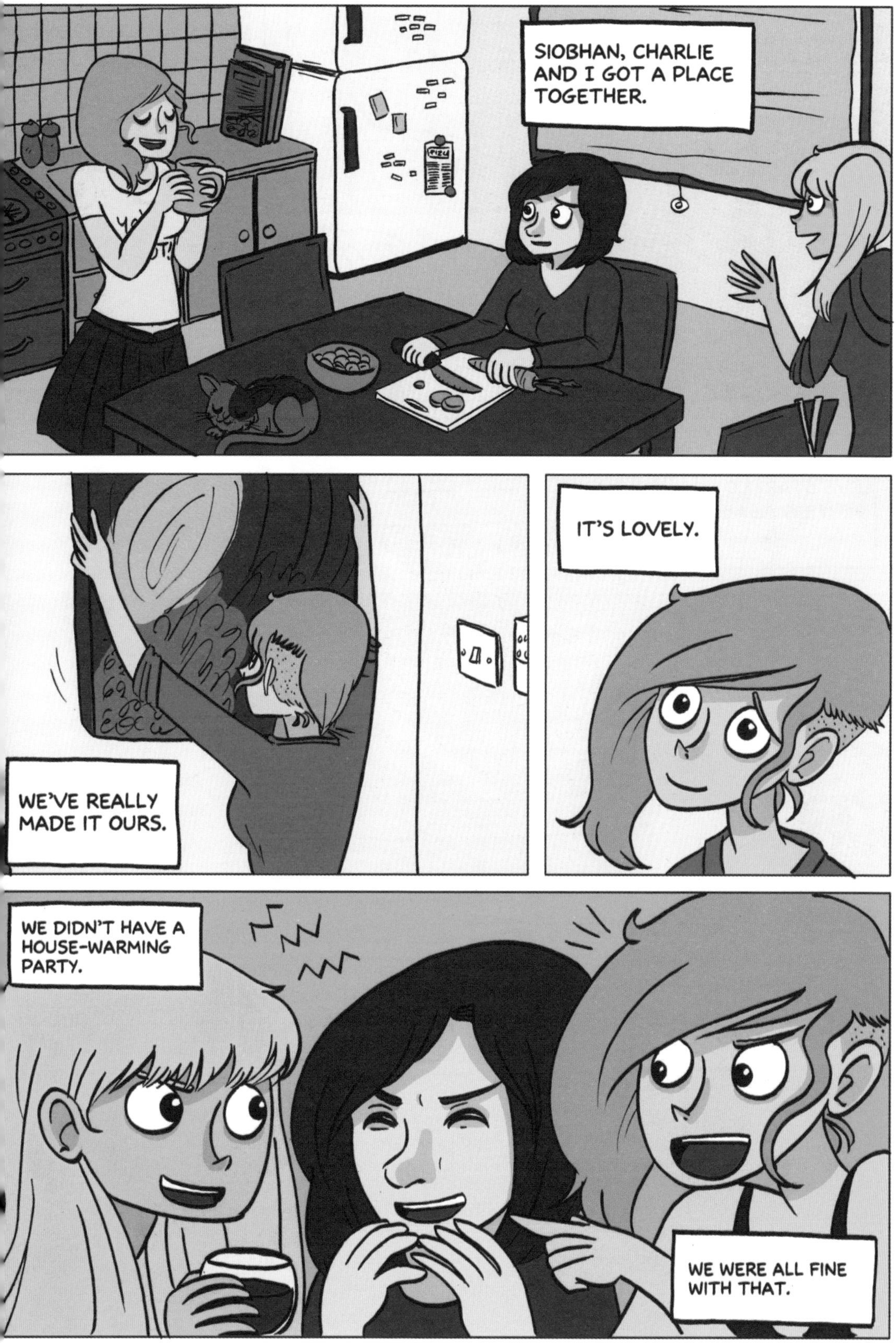
SIOBHAN, CHARLIE AND I GOT A PLACE TOGETHER.
WE'VE REALLY MADE IT OURS.
IT'S LOVELY.
WE DIDN'T HAVE A HOUSE-WARMING PARTY.
WE WERE ALL FINE WITH THAT.

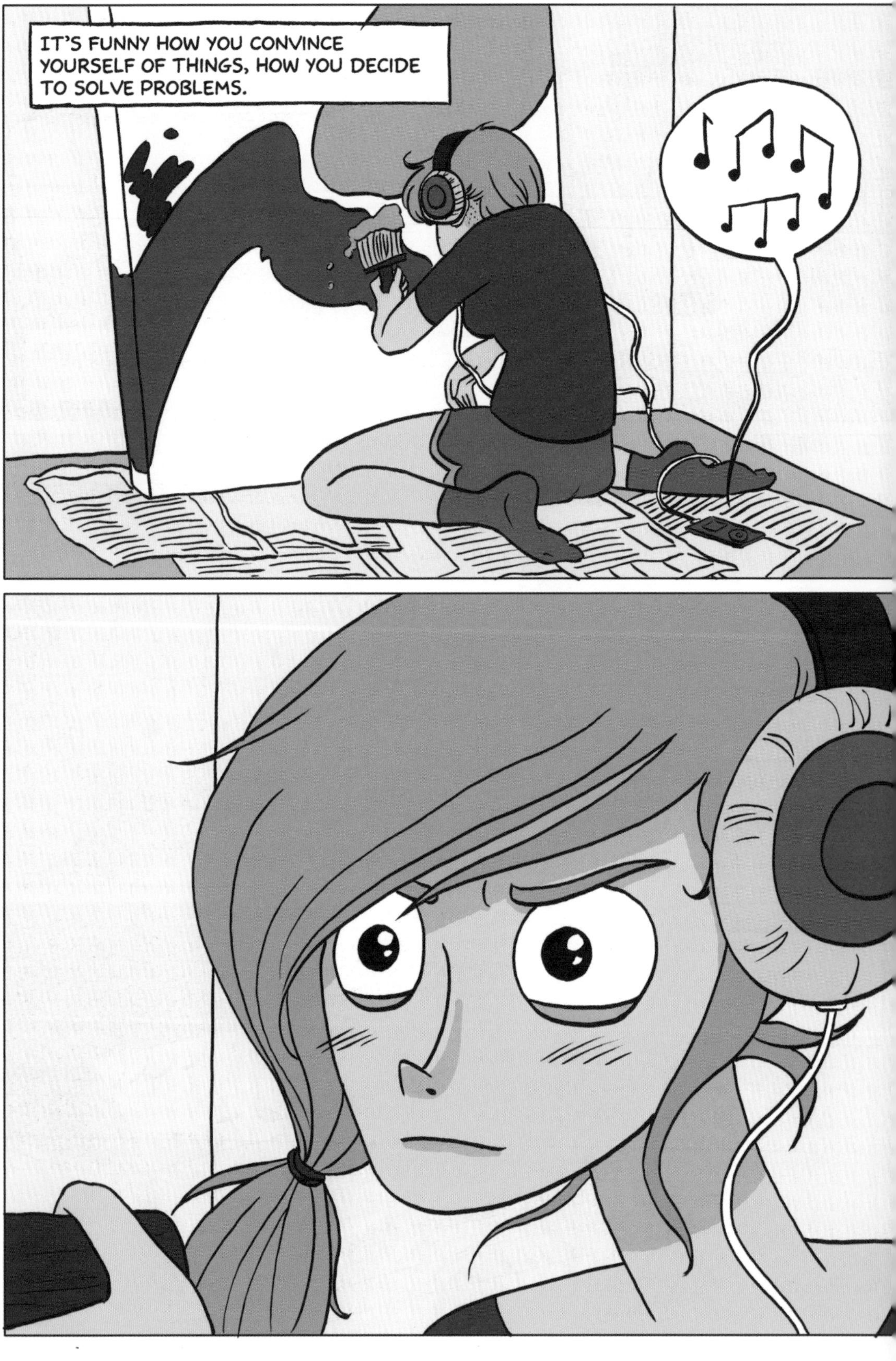
IT'S FUNNY HOW YOU CONVINCE YOURSELF OF THINGS, HOW YOU DECIDE TO SOLVE PROBLEMS.

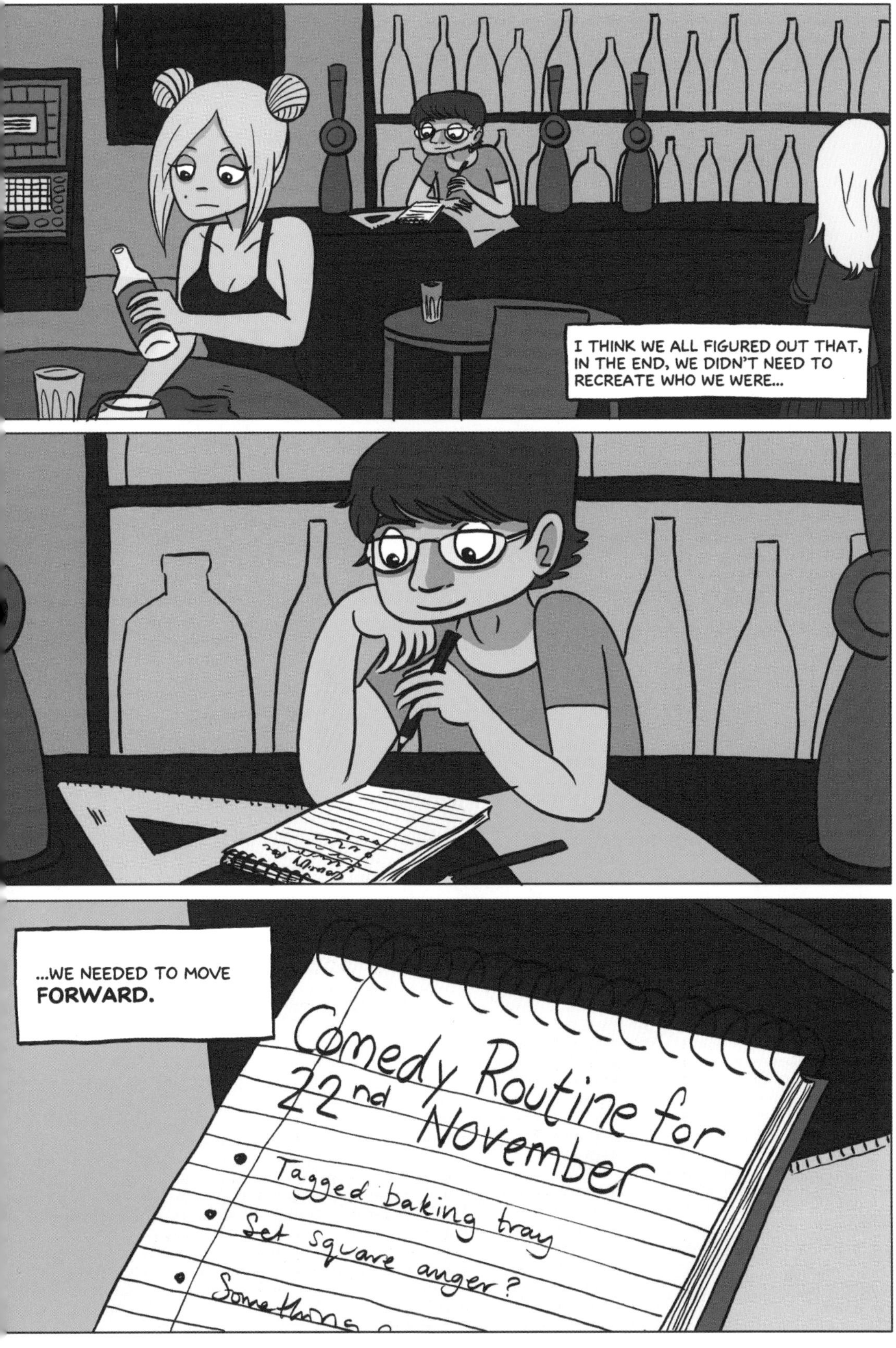
I THINK WE ALL FIGURED OUT THAT, IN THE END, WE DIDN'T NEED TO RECREATE WHO WE WERE...
...WE NEEDED TO MOVE **FORWARD.**
Comedy Routine for 22nd November
Tagged baking tray
Set square anger?

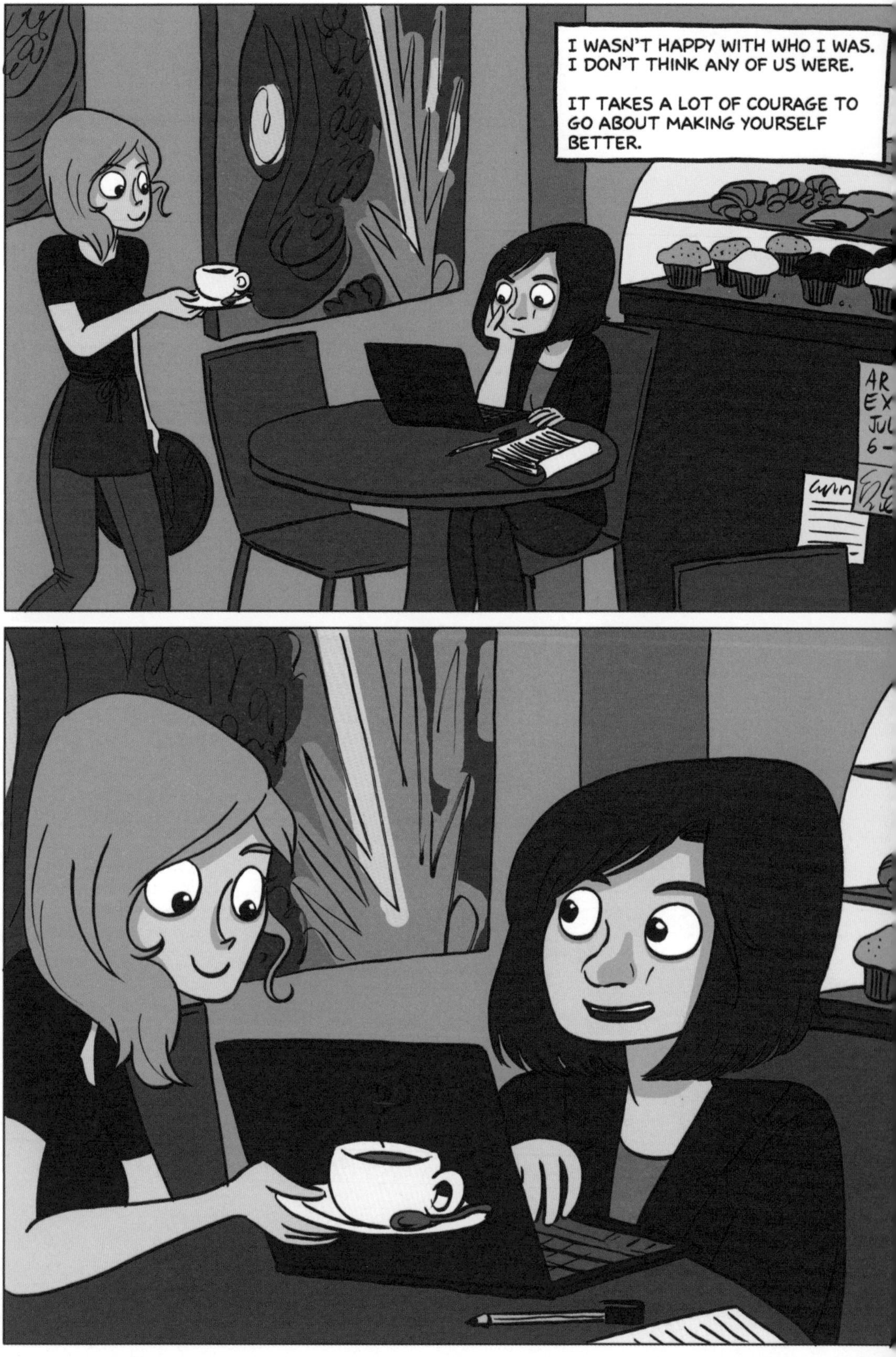
I WASN'T HAPPY WITH WHO I WAS. I DON'T THINK ANY OF US WERE.
IT TAKES A LOT OF COURAGE TO GO ABOUT MAKING YOURSELF BETTER.

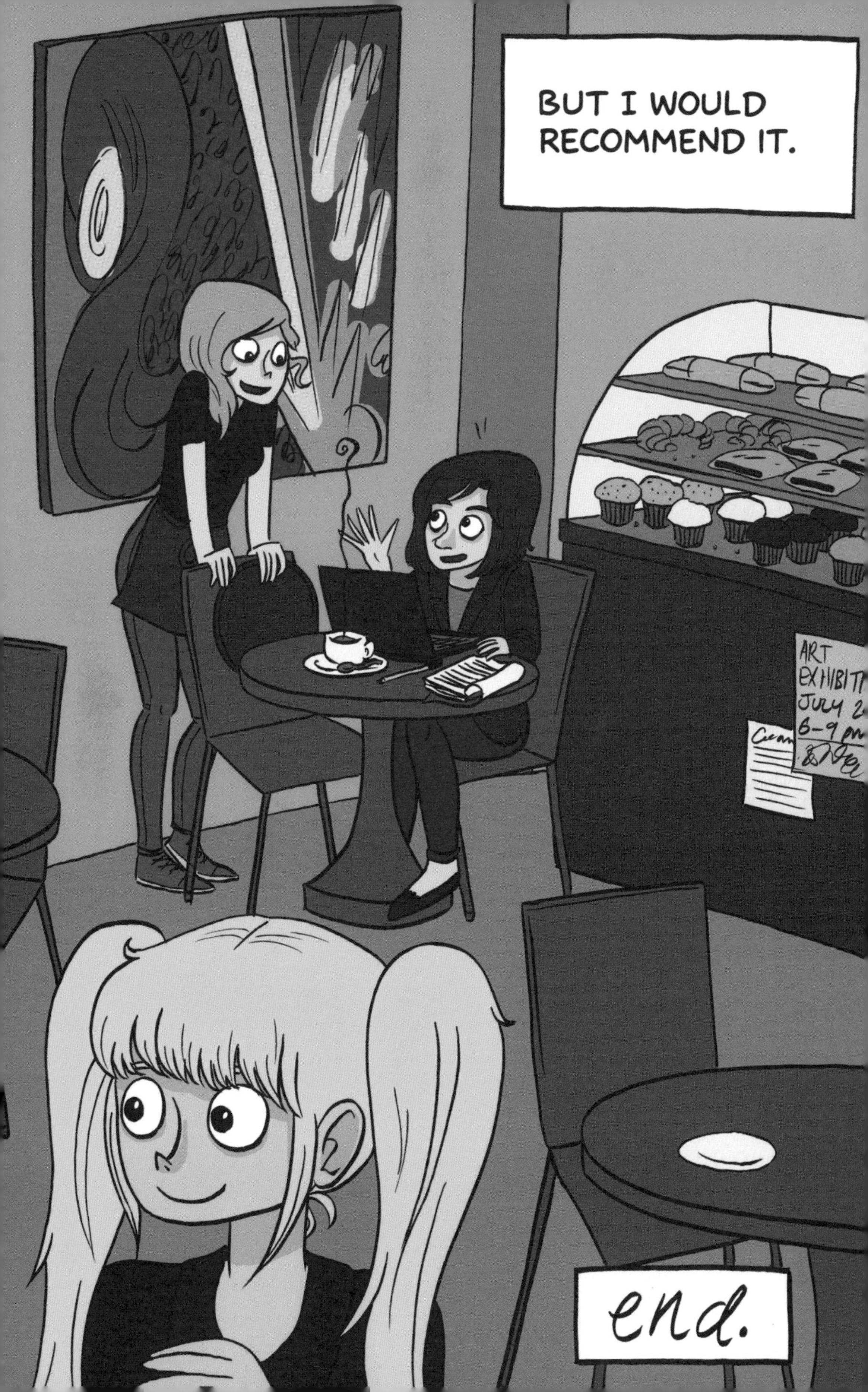
BUT I WOULD RECOMMEND IT.
end.

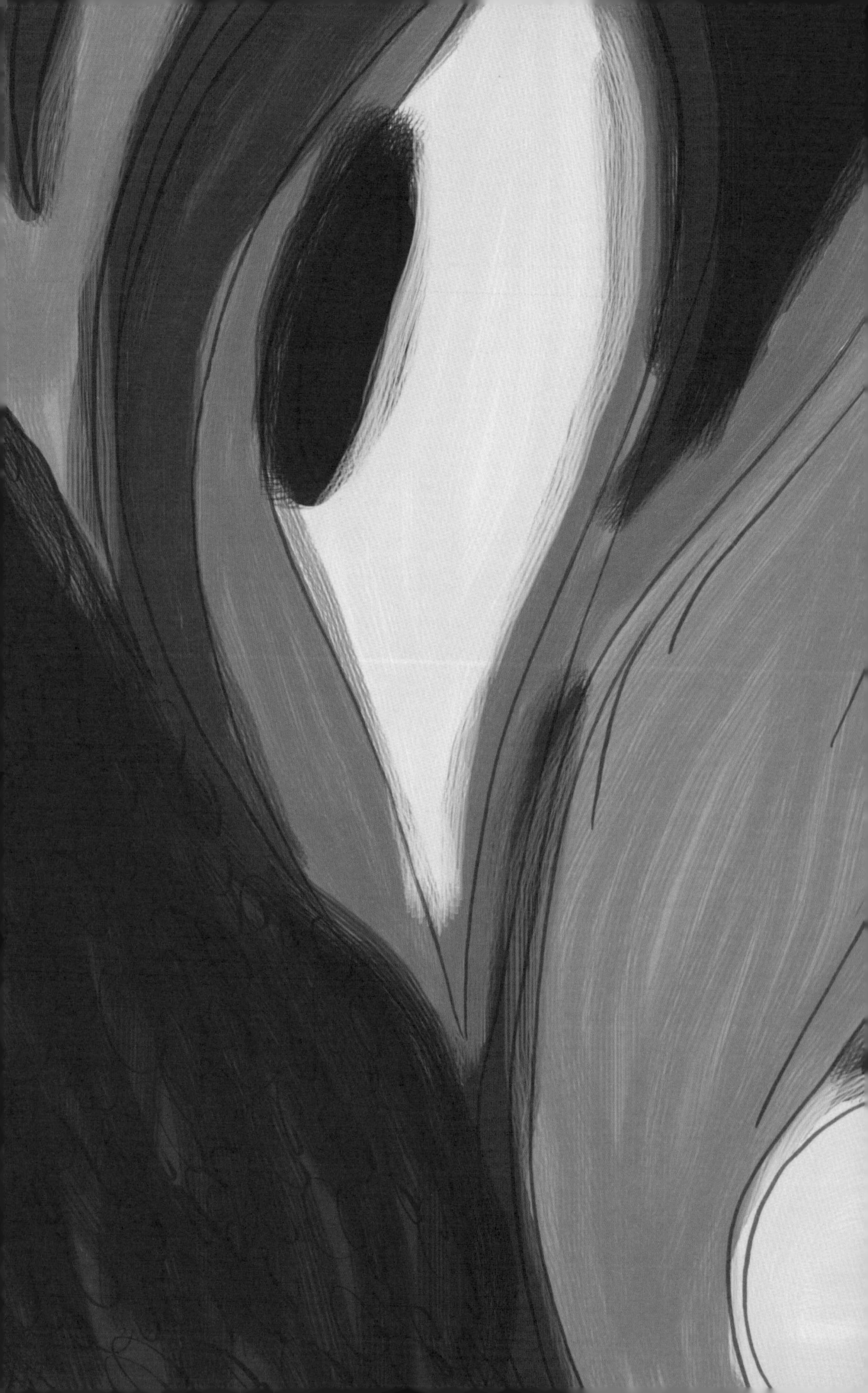

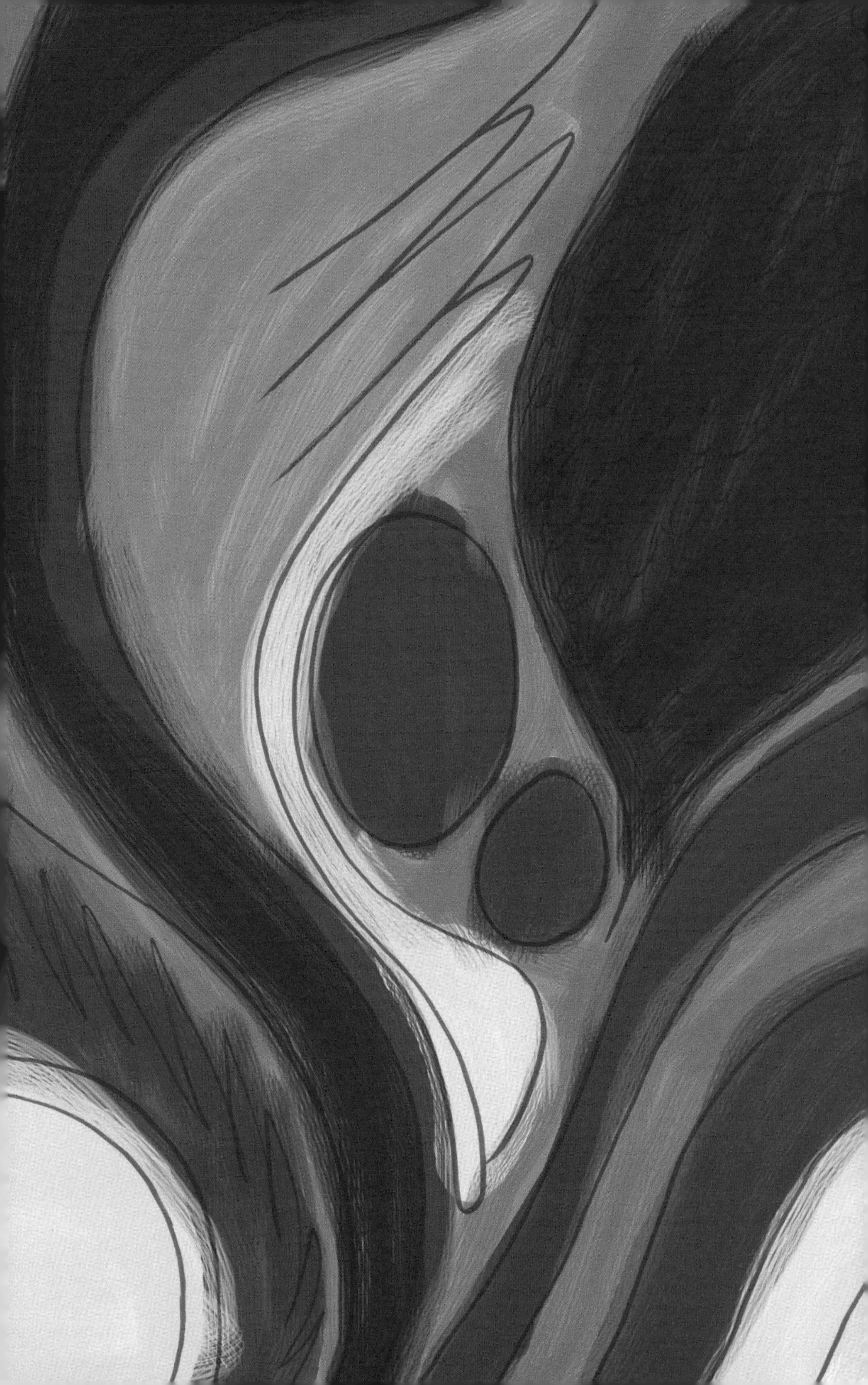

GUEST ART GALLERY

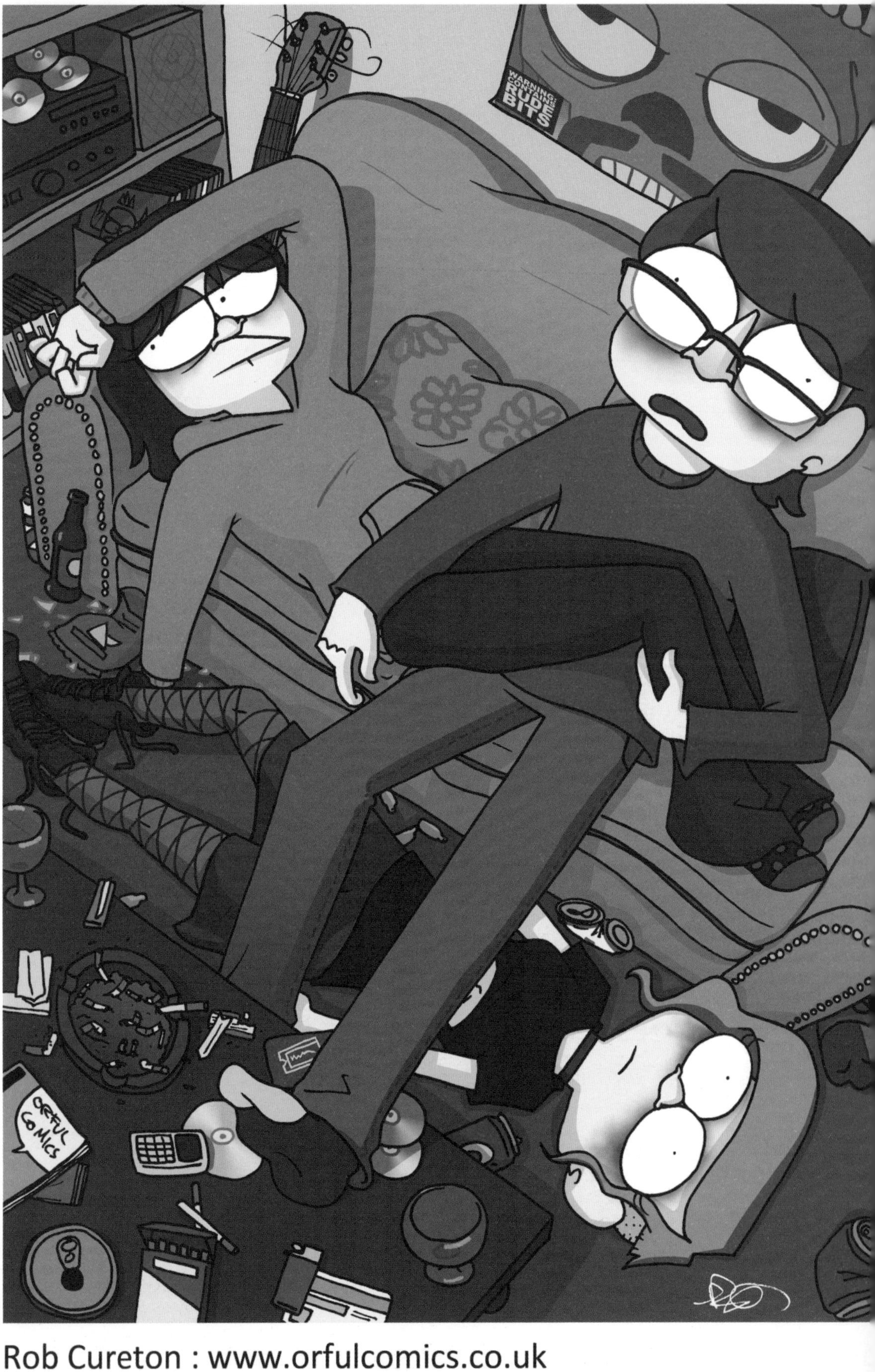
WARNING: CONTAINS: RUDE BITS
ORFUL COMICS

Rob Cureton : www.orfulcomics.co.uk

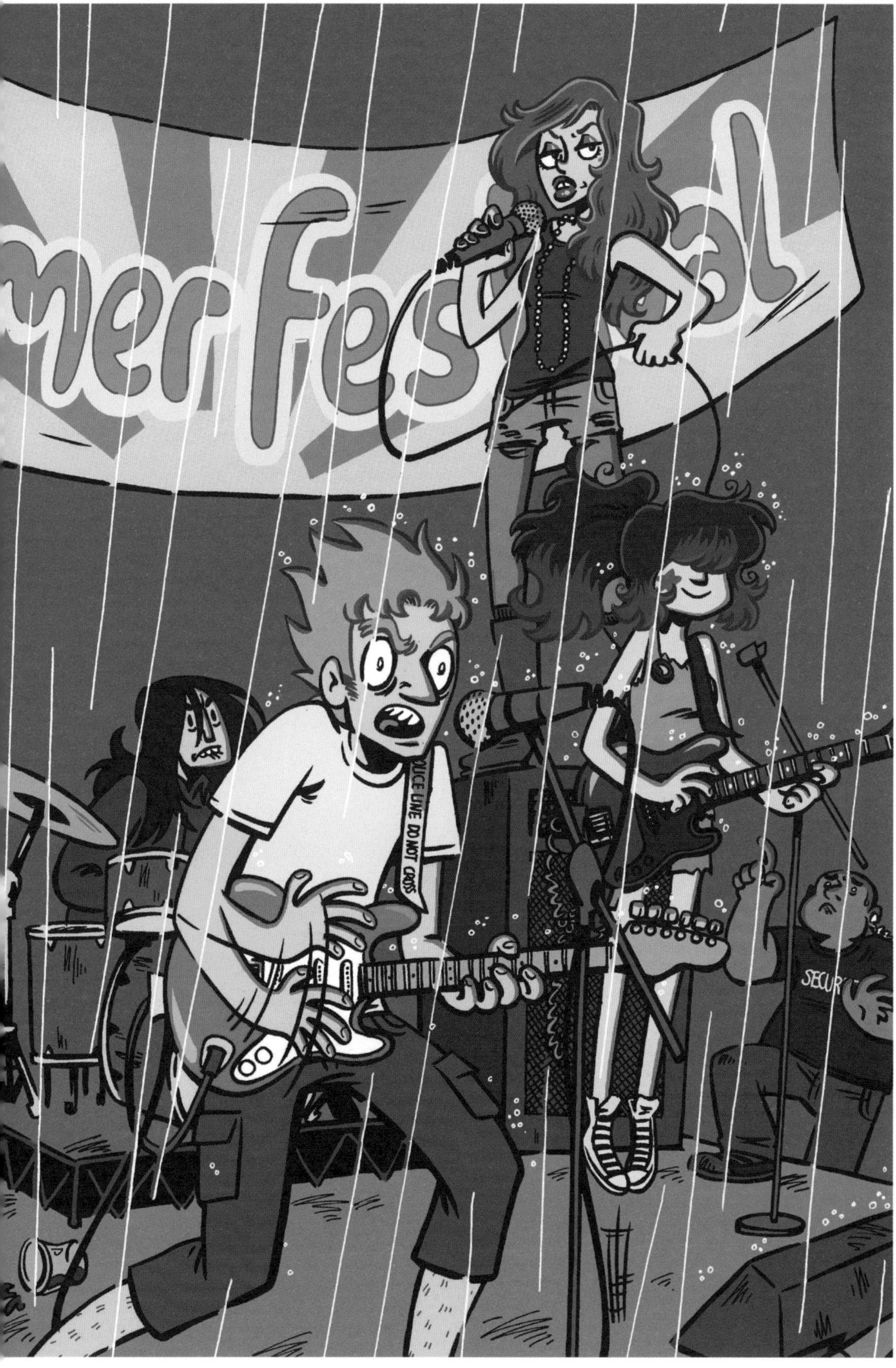
merFes
POLICE LINE DO NOT CROSS
SECUR

ammy Borras : sammyborras.blogspot.co.uk

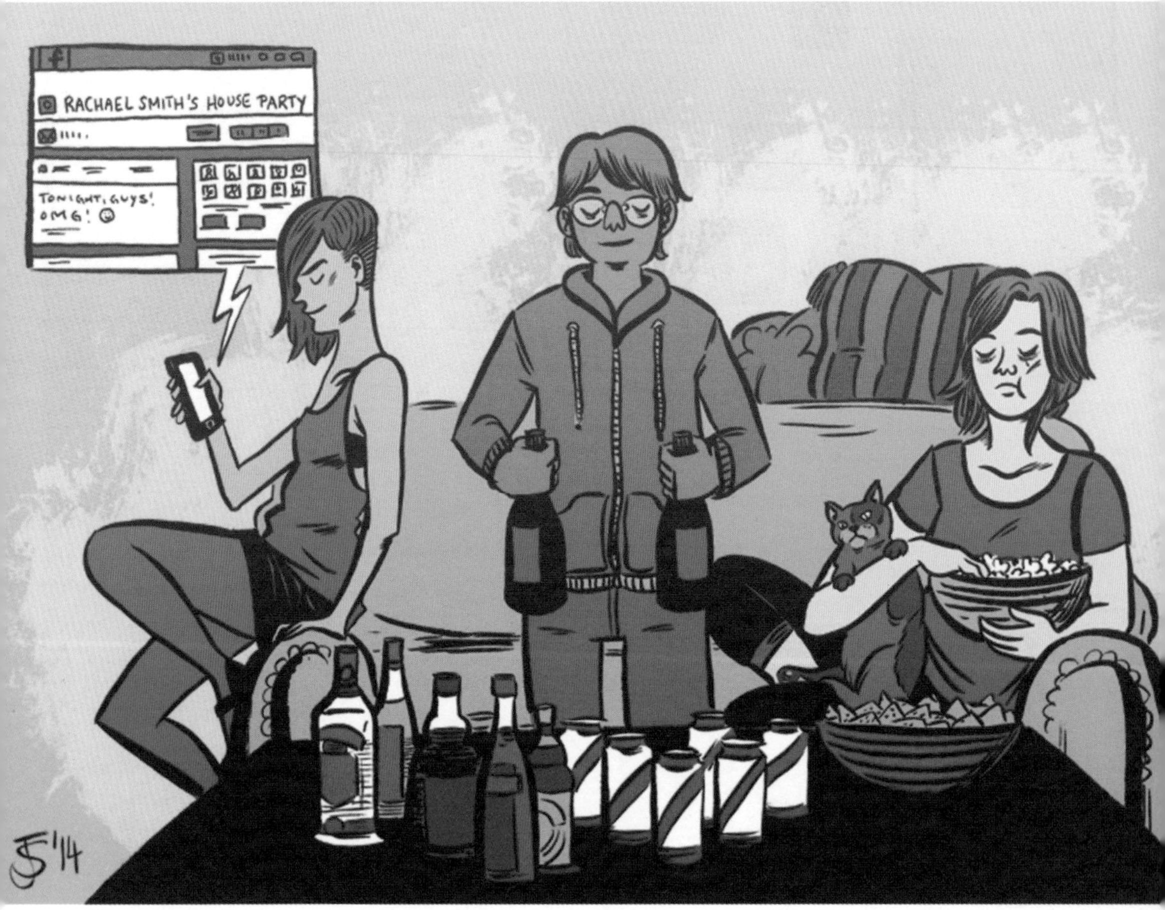
RACHAEL SMITH'S HOUSE PARTY
TONIGHT, GUYS!
OMG!
JS '14

Julia Scheele : www.juliascheele.co.uk

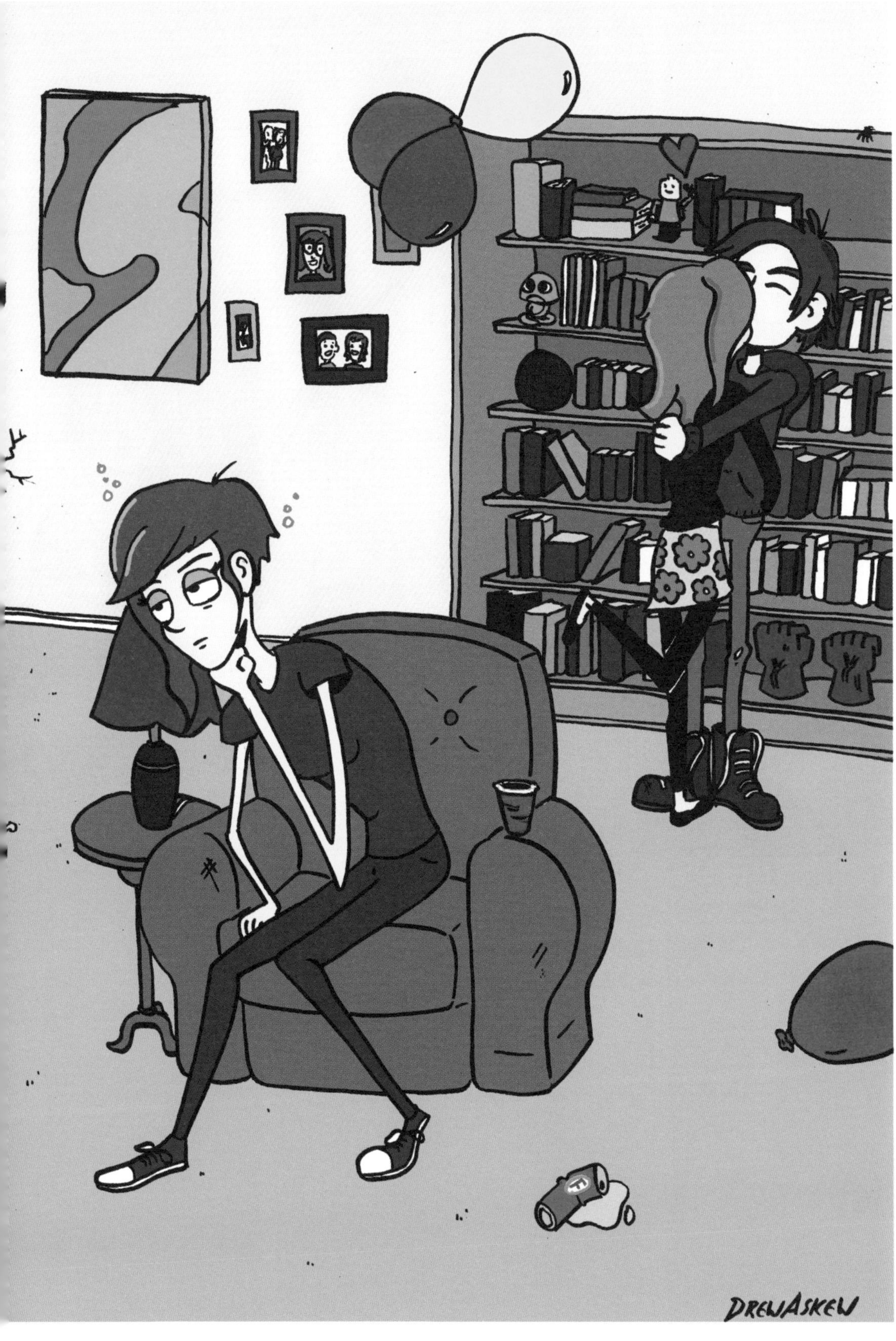
DREWASKEW

rew Askew : haveagoherocomic.blogspot.co.uk

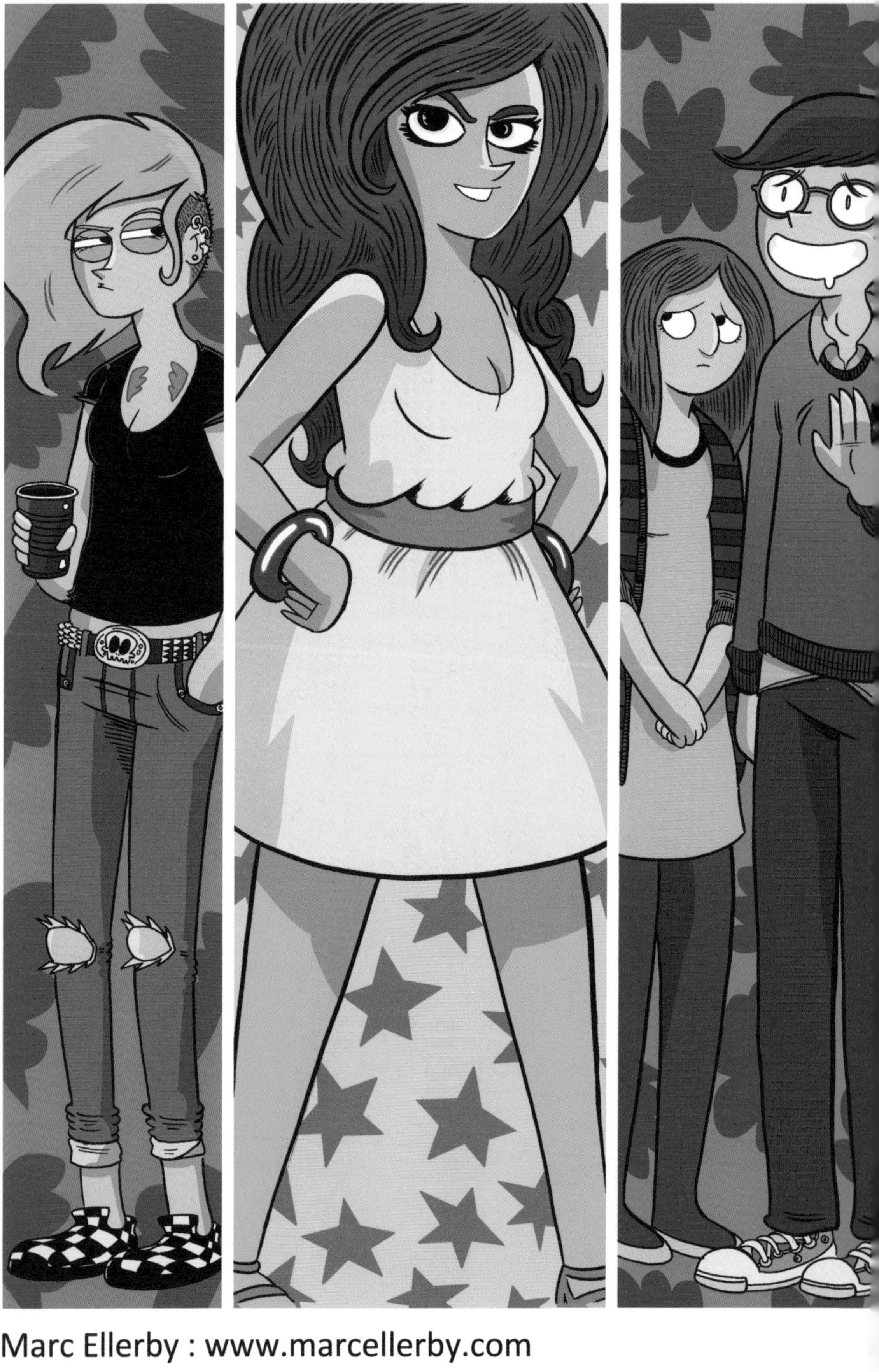

Marc Ellerby : www.marcellerby.com

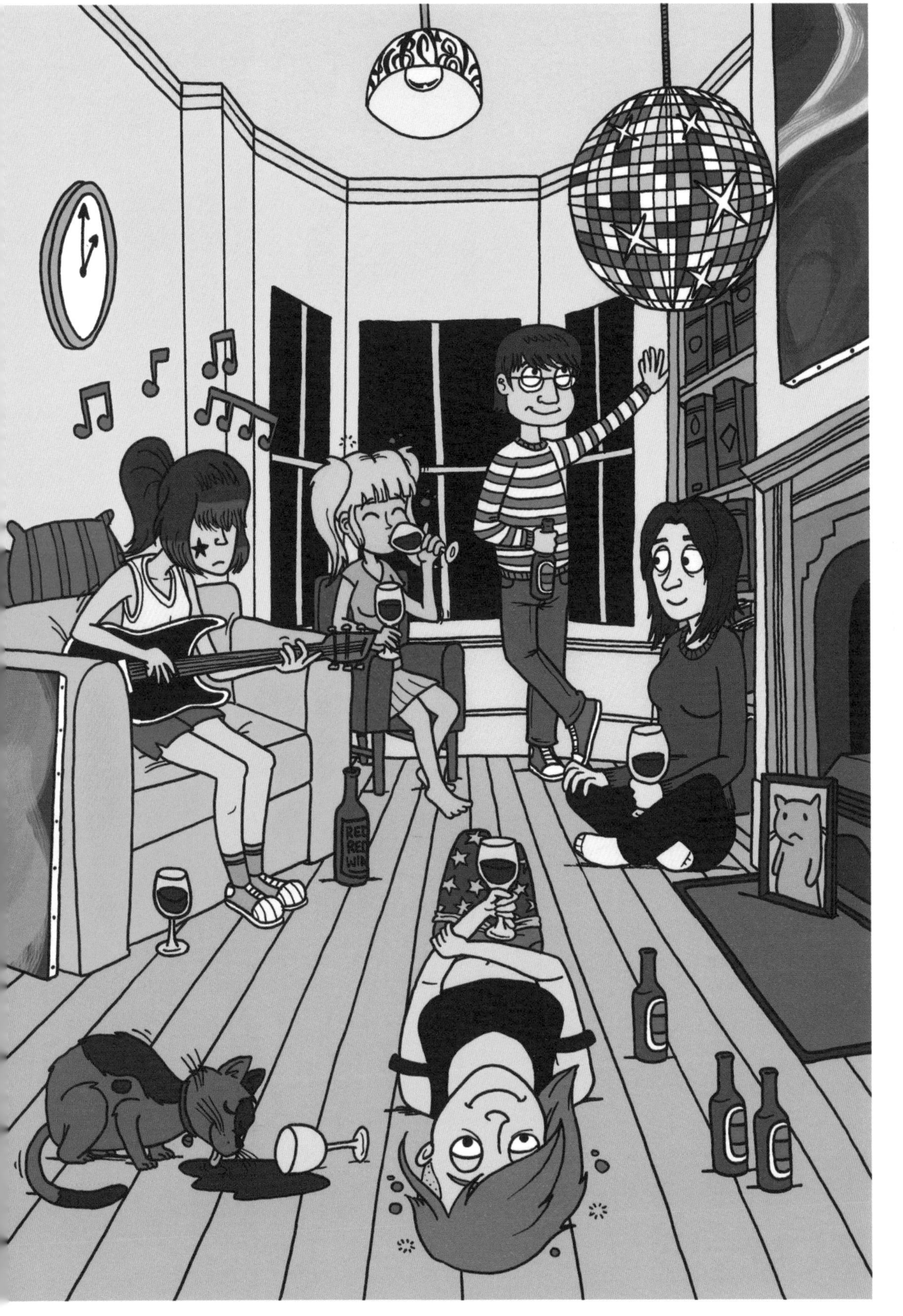

aul Shinn : www.paulshinndraws.com

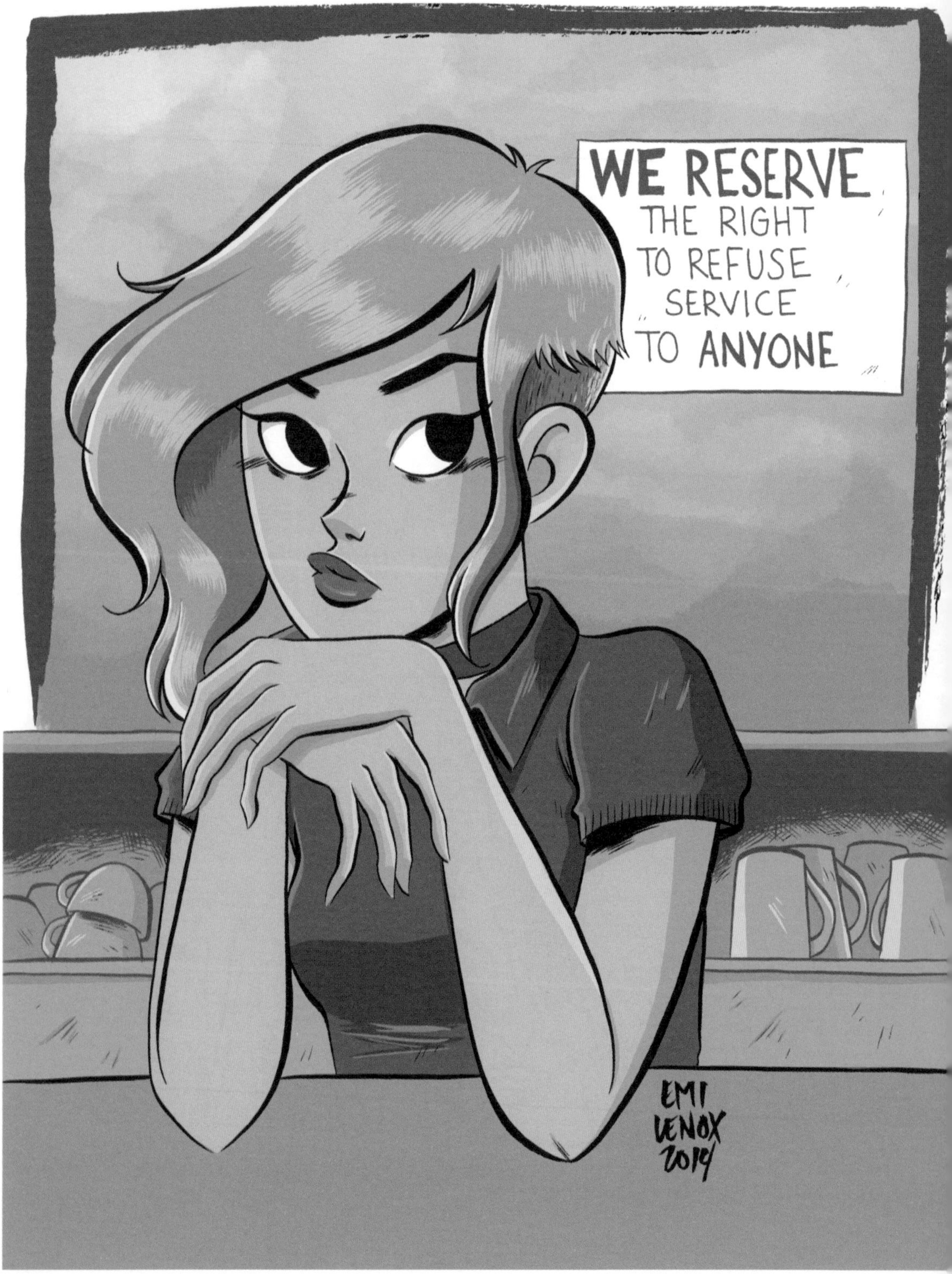
WE RESERVE
THE RIGHT
TO REFUSE
SERVICE
TO ANYONE
EMI
LENOX
2019

Emi Lenox : emilenox.wordpress.com

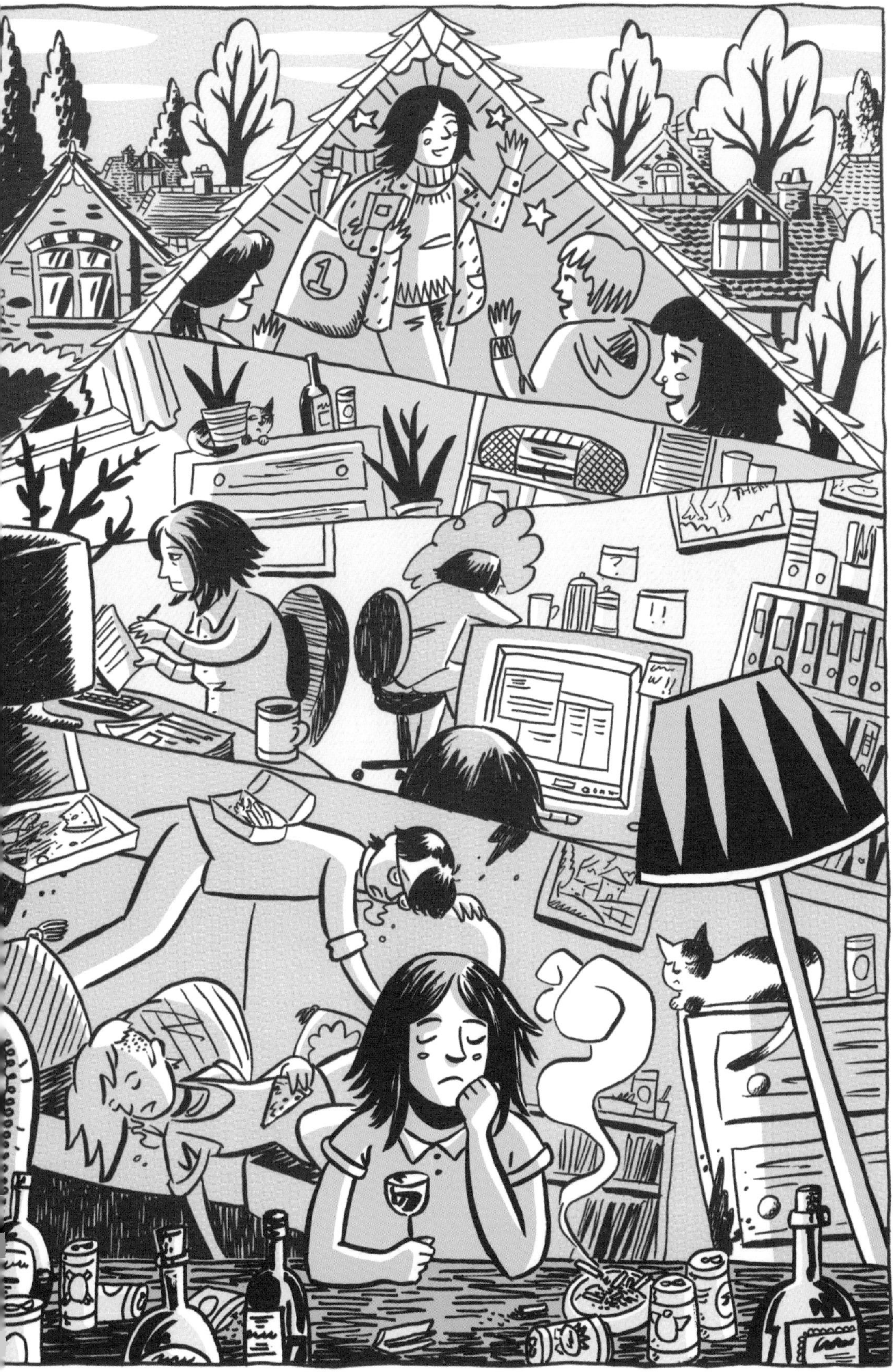

JohnCei 2014

ohn Cei Douglas : johnceidouglas.tumblr.com

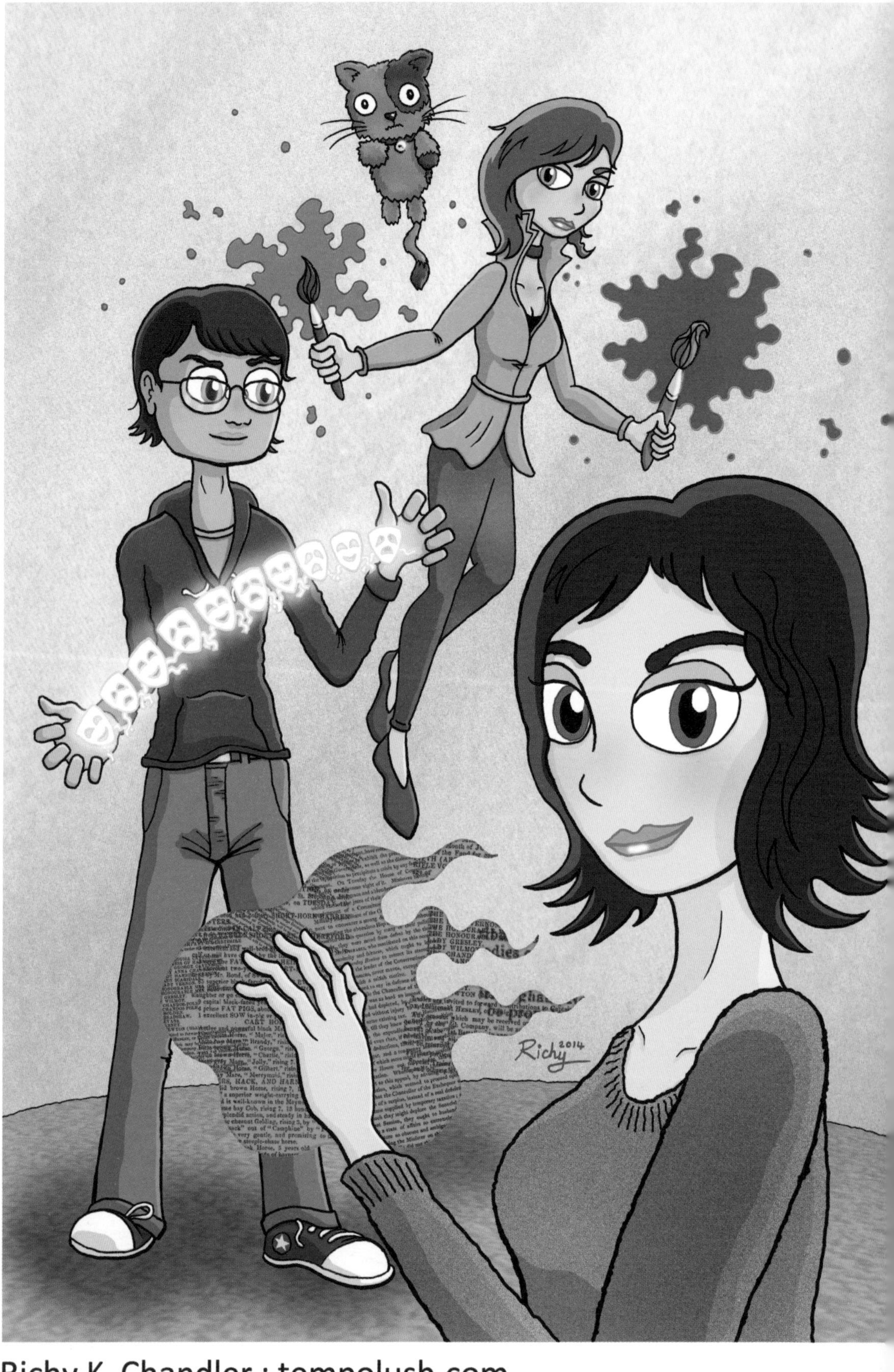
Richy 2014

Richy K. Chandler : tempolush.com

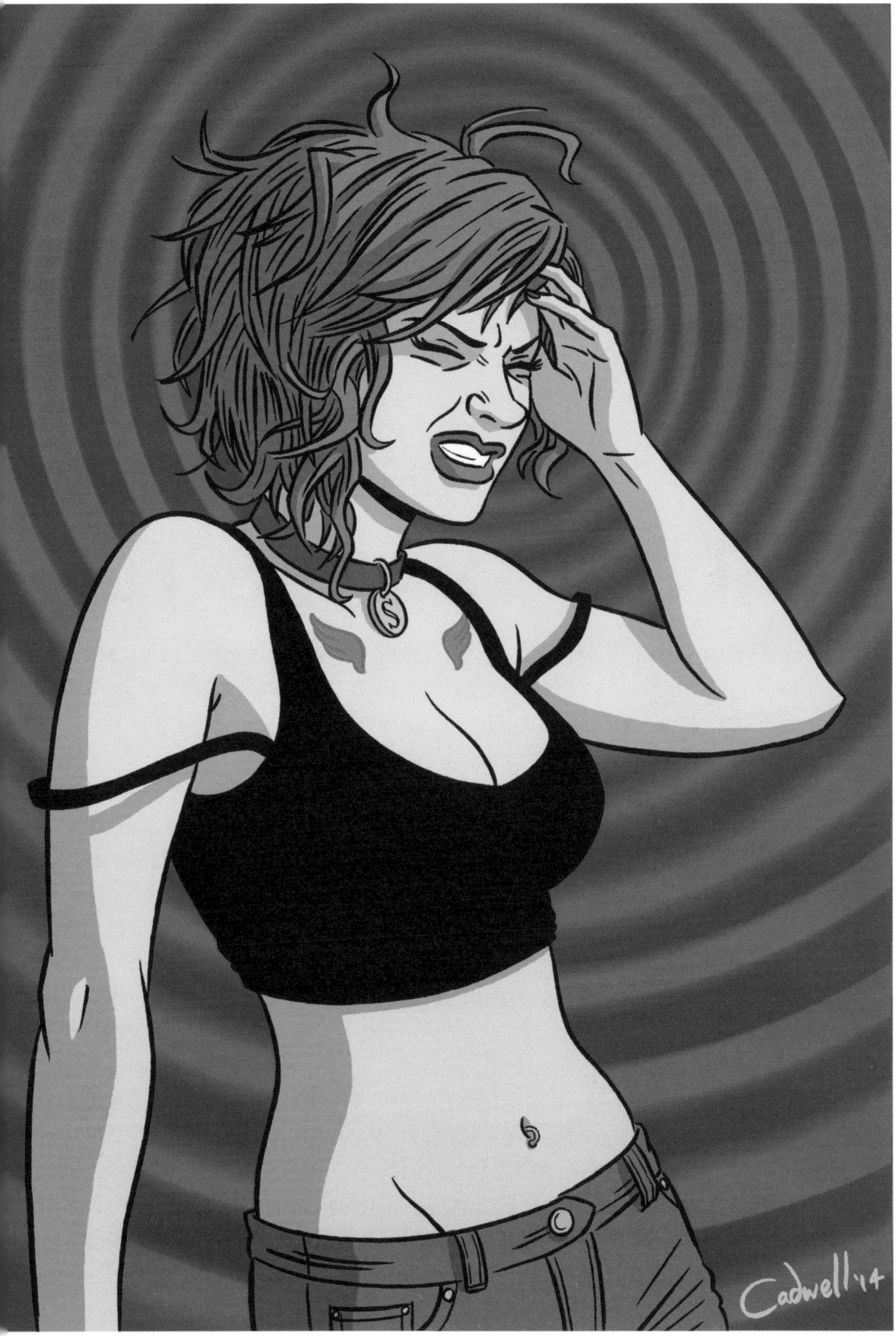
Cadwell '14

ɟdam Cadwell : www.adamcadwell.com

SPECIAL THANKS TO

Adam Cadwell, Marc Ellerby, Paul Shinn, Rob Cureton,
Richy K Chandler, Isabel Greenberg, Sammy Borras,
John Cei Douglas, Julia Scheele, Drew Askew, Emi Lenox,
Adam Weikert, Tiernan Welch, Emma Craig-West, Kara Smith,
James Shrig, Andy Leeke, Paul Banks, Cyrus Kent, Selina Lock,
Jay Eales, Andy Waterfield, Jeni Simpson, my amazing family,
and anyone who has ever bought one of my comics or told me I
was doing OK - you're all rad.

ALSO! THANKS TO

Spencer King, Elliot Baggott, WolfZombie, Nathan Human,
Lynsey, Julian Black, Hollie Eden, kane, Justin Pearson, John C.,
Becky Donovan, Sara Westrop, Will Brooker, Cam Mezé,
Matthew Sims, Kerry Wilkinson, Marc Staniford, Louise Jenkins,
Rodrigo Villaseñor, Matthew Robson, Tony Coleman, Adrian
Manning, TONY BACIC, Simon O'Reilly, Paul Braidford, Stephen
Molloy, Sarah Millman, Wendy Wildey, Greg Smyth, Andy
Warrington, Chris Budd, Alex Dawson, Kate Dickson, Sean
McCarthy, Andy Oliver, Alan Henderson, Christopher Mills, Bob
Turner, Paddy Johnston, Louie, Sarah McIntyre, Nikki Stu, Adam
Snape, Grant Jobes, Reza tootoonchian, Simon Siddall, Saiyda
Adalat, Andy Reeves, Kyle Miller, Sarah Zaidan, Paul Wright,
Graham Muir, Andy Salkeld, Steven Lomax, James Scott, kirk,
Kimberly Riddell, Corinna Vigier, Jake Betancourt-Laverde, Sean
Canning, Nigel Uzzell, sean holden, Ian Hall, Oli Jacobs, William
Kavanagh, Lucinda Burnett, Bryan Poerner, Matthew Wiese, Alex
Ingram, Johanna, John Sanders, Craig Scott, Will Yeomans,
Fredrick E Thomas, Adriane Ruzak, Ali Safavi, Jessicca Moore,
lloydie, Jonny Bull, David Campbell, Stephen Quinn

TRINA GROSVENOR, Jason Lock, Richard Price, Tom Shapira, Angela Boyle, Charles Haydn-Slater, Karl Topping, Dean Simons, Hannah Howden, Freddie Mould-Cook, Andrew James, Jon Low, James Walker, insanity prawnboy 23, abdulaziz jeeran, Revek, Matthew Benter, Emma Fairgrieve, Elias N Vasylenko, Robert Shimizu, mike thomas, Vincent Graves, Steven Bakker, Steve Lomax, Francois PALLIER, Bob Ferry, and everyone else who very kindly pledged to the Kickstarter project - you guys made this book a reality.

You GUYS ARE THE FUCKIN' BEST

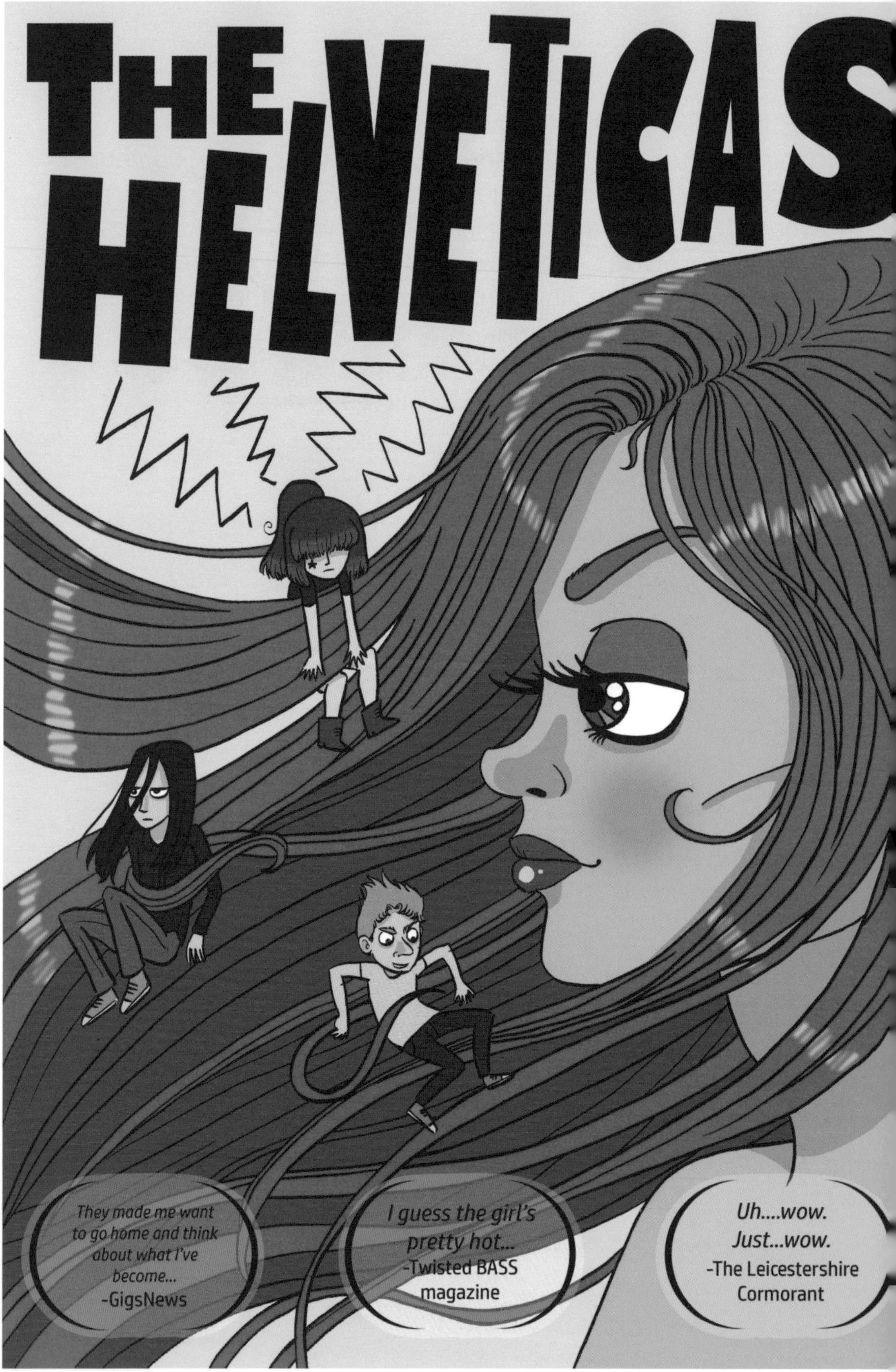
THE HELVETICAS
They made me want to go home and think about what I've become... -GigsNews
I guess the girl's pretty hot... -Twisted BASS magazine
Uh....wow. Just...wow. -The Leicestershire Cormorant

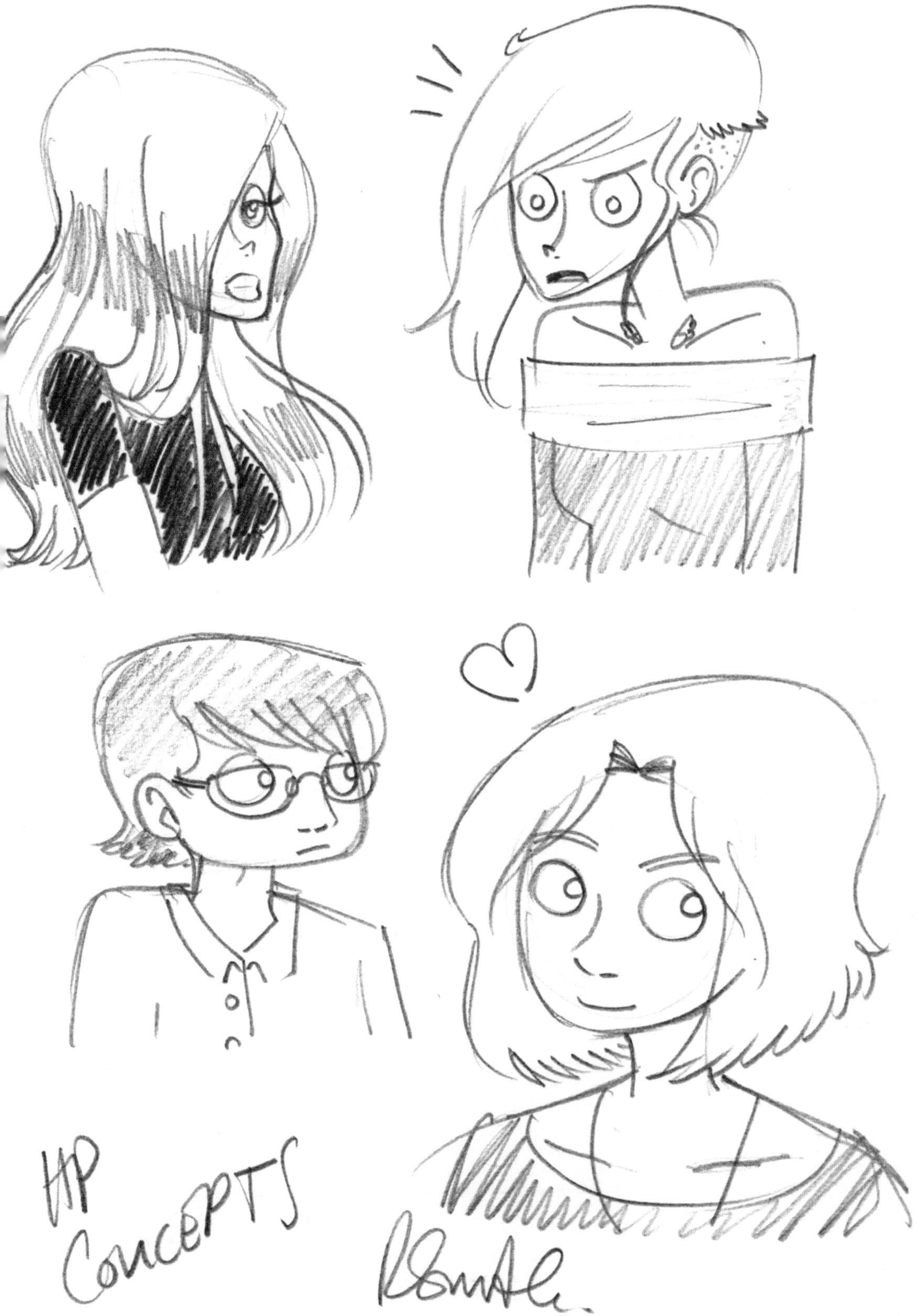
HP CONCEPTS

Artist portrait – by Isabel Greenberg

Rachael Smith is an illustrator/comic artist/writer
currently living in Leicester, UK.
'House Party' is her debut graphic novel, and follows
'The Way We Write', 'I Am Fire', and
'Flimsy's Guide to Modern Living'.

Rachael also has a diary comic called
'One Good Thing' and a Q&A blog for her character
Flimsy called 'Ask Flimsy'.

www.rachaelsmith.org
www.etsy.com/uk/shop/FlimsyKitten
www.rachaelsonegoodthing.blogspot.com.uk
www.askflimsy.tumblr.com

Twitter: @rachael_